SEASONS
a year of fabulous food

ANNABELLE WHITE

contents

introduction

Eating good, simple food with friends and family is one of life's greatest joys. Sitting around the table and sharing fresh seasonal ingredients with little fuss is the ideal. No sumptuous meal eaten alone can ever be as memorable as a simple repast with great company. An omelette, for example, with a crisp seasonal salad and great bread can be heavenly with someone dear to you.

Like so many things, the less you do to many foods and produce, the better. Rather than complicated procedures, think a quick chargrill or steamed fresh asparagus rather than making it into a cream soup, sauce, timbale, mousseline or anything in aspic. Leave that to chefs in fancy restaurants.

Our produce stores and seasonal foods need to be more celebrated; we take so much for granted. Get excited about strawberries in spring, vine-ripened tomatoes in January, whitebait in September/October, new season's apples in the autumn and stone fruits in the midst of hot languid, summer days. Forget fresh tomatoes in June and think tamarillos in winter, not imported berries.

This was the main motivating force behind this cookbook. You, the home cooks of New Zealand, have given me the necessary direction. You want simple, everyday recipes, not complicated methods, using ingredients on hand (in other words, a quick look in your pantry, rather than numerous trips to food suppliers), and any cook of any ability could give it a go!

Cooks quickly give me feedback about favourite dishes. This cookbook is a collection of these treasured recipes. This is my seventh cookbook and every time I sit down to collate these recipes and tips, I think I'm writing this for you, a cooking companion – someone who will treasure, appreciate and find this cook's journal of jottings useful. Take it to bed to read as the seasons unfold and use it in the kitchen rather than placing it on the coffee table. If the book gets stained and ragged looking after a few weeks, that's another joy!

This book covers a year of travel, seasonal food, tips and advice. In no way is it intended to be a comprehensive seasonal cookbook, but hopefully one that encourages you further, especially to try new ways with traditional favourite vegetables and perhaps to try something new, such as witlof or Puy lentils.

My whole-hearted thanks for making this cook's journal possible must go to Mr Brett Newell and José Hernandez of Eurowine; Countess Roselyne de Casteja of Veuve Clicquot Ponsardin in Reims, France; the South Australian Tourism Commission; Astrid Mulholland-Licht of the Austrian National Tourist Office based in Sydney; Bruce Campbell and all the team at Mainland Products; Diana Marbeck, the former senior account manager for Chatelle Brandy; Lloyd Anderson of News Media; Karl van den Brink of Brink's Chicken; the team at Penguin Books; chef James Archibald and my parents, John and Jacqueline White, who are my neighbours and constant support; Jacqui and Phil Dixon and the Sabato team for great products; and speaking of other great products – Jenny Myers and everyone at Gourmet Direct.

No cookbook would inspire without photography, and a special thanks to photographer Kieran Scott for encouraging me and giving me the confidence to get busy 'taking snaps' throughout the year and to help me with the essence of this book, and also to Scott Venning for photography as well. Special thanks also to chef and caterer Nicola Hudson for her passion for great food and her unflagging assistance – she is a complete joy to work with in a busy kitchen.

Finally, this book is dedicated to Graeme Moran: for his constant support and willingness to sample and review a myriad of dishes – making hours in the kitchen even more pleasurable, and for his honesty, insightfulness, sensitivity, empathy, patience, love and care – I couldn't have done this without him! Thank you.

Annabelle White
Birkenhead Point

JANUARY ... *berries & seeing old friends*

Intimacy and pleasure can be found in the simplest ways. Sitting quietly after the frenetic festive season and devouring a bowl of fresh raspberries embellished only with a kiss of cold, thick cream is highly recommended. If you would like to cement this relationship further into a wondrous marriage of flavours, add a hint of chocolate – it's a berry special relationship – there is something quite remarkable about that strong sharp sweetness of the raspberry combined with a rich coating of chocolate. That's why there are so many chocolate desserts on menus with a raspberry coulis.

Ever wondered what a coulis really is? It's a culinary term, or chef speak, for a thick purée or sauce – a tomato coulis can be as common as a berry coulis. To make a raspberry coulis: process 1kg raspberries with 1 cup sugar; strain to remove the seeds, then flavour with your favourite liqueur. The coulis will keep for up to 2 weeks in the fridge or 2–3 months frozen. It's wonderful with pancakes, ice-cream, meringues, cakes and sweet tarts.

Selecting framboise (otherwise known as crème de framboise or raspberry liqueur) would intensify the whole process completely.

Don't be shy about adding berries to a favourite, fresh fruit cake or simply as an irresistible topping for a chocolate cake – see page 9 for inspiration. Drizzle your favourite chocolate cake with a rich, thin, chocolate icing and top with fresh berries. So get a little raspberry crazy ...

BERRY BITES

* Buy raspberries with a dry, velvety texture. Avoid any with excess juice or any sight of mould. Keep in the fridge and do not wash, just spread onto kitchen towels and pick off any dirt.

* Raspberry yoghurt ice-cream is a creamy ice delight with full flavour. Place 1kg plain yoghurt, 300g frozen raspberries, 1/4 cup lemon or lime juice and 1 cup sugar in the bowl of an ice-cream machine and churn until frozen yoghurt appears. Delicious just like that with fresh raspberries or freeze and serve as ice-cream.

* Raspberries also feature superbly in a sauce to accompany duck. For the sauce place 3 cups raspberries in a pot with 1 chopped tomato, 1 tblsp tomato paste, 3 tblsp raspberry vinegar, a bay leaf, a few sprigs of fresh thyme and a few stems of parsley. Simmer on low heat until the juice of the berries is released. Pour the berry mixture into a sieve and press down with a spatula to release all the juices back into the saucepan. Place the saucepan over the heat, add duck stock (about 1/4 cup) and simmer. You then add crème de cassis for extra flavour, and some cooks add a little sugar syrup (boil equal parts sugar and water together) to reach desired sweetness, but honey and crème de cassis will do the trick!

* To make raspberry vinegar, just crush 500g raspberries and place them in a ceramic or glass bowl (not aluminium). Pour over 2 cups white wine or red wine vinegar and leave overnight. Next day strain the liquid into a heatproof jar and add 2 cups (500g) sugar. Stand the jar in a saucepan until water comes halfway up the sides of the jar. Simmer for an hour, then strain the raspberry vinegar into sterilised jars. It's ready to use immediately, but becomes mellow and lovely as the months go by!

* Raspberries and peaches go superbly together. Just pour boiling water over 6 peaches in a bowl, leave 3 minutes, then peel. Place equal amounts of sugar and water — for example, 2 cups water and 2 cups sugar — in a pot and simmer 5 minutes until slightly thickened. Place whole, peeled peaches in a bowl with 300g raspberries. Pour over syrup. Refrigerate. Serve one peach with berries per person and spoon a little syrup over the fruit.

* Make a raspberry batter pudding. Make a smooth batter of 11/4 cups milk, 2 eggs, 1 cup flour and 1/4 cup sugar. Add 15g melted butter, blending in slowly and then well with a whisk. Leave for 60 minutes. Melt an additional 15g butter and place in a 25cm baking dish, add 2 cups fresh raspberries and sprinkle with 1/4 cup sugar. Sprinkle over a little liqueur of your choice. Pour batter over fruit. Bake at 200°C for 30 minutes, then turn down the oven to 150°C for the last 10 minutes to prevent over-browning. Serve the pudding at once with a dusting of icing or caster sugar and ice-cream and cream.

* Make a great summer drink with crushed raspberries, fresh lime juice, framboise, vodka and ice. Great colour and great flavour!

JOHN'S SIMPLY DELICIOUS RASPBERRY MUFFINS

These are the perfect breakfast treat for friends. The fresh raspberries explode delicious fruit flavours in your mouth and I love to serve them just warm with a light dusting of icing sugar and lots of hot coffee. This recipe was given to me by my very good friend, John Borwick, who whips these up for breakfast at Evergreen Lodge in Queenstown.

11/2 cups self-raising flour
1/2 cup flour
1/2 cup caster sugar
1 cup desiccated coconut
3/4 cup canola oil
3/4 cup buttermilk
1/4 cup milk
1 large egg
1 cup raspberries

METHOD

Place the dry ingredients into a bowl and mix well. In another bowl combine the oil, buttermilk, milk and egg. Add the wet to the dry ingredients and blend until just combined, adding the raspberries at the last minute. Place in large muffin tins and fan bake for 20 minutes at 200°C, then turn down to 150°C for another 10 minutes.

Remove from oven and leave to rest for a few minutes, then while still warm dust with icing sugar and serve.

* If you are using frozen raspberries you may need extra cooking time. Allow another 5 minutes in the 'turned off' oven if they are not completely cooked.

'Life is uncertain. Eat dessert first.' ERNESTINE ULMER

ALI'S CHOCOLATE COCONUT SLICE

One day the funny and delightfully charming TVNZ presenter Alison Mau turned up in the kitchen to film at the house for a segment of 'Home Front'. A busy mother of two, she was rushing with the crew and didn't have time for breakfast. I gave her two pieces of this delicious chocolate slice and she was in heaven. Since then, it's been known as Ali's slice.

Serve this divine slice with a bowl of raspberries for a great celebration of summer. The intense chocolate flavour will be enhanced by the zing of the raspberries. Please note, there are no eggs in this recipe.

250g butter
1 cup sugar
2 tblsp cocoa
1 tblsp golden syrup
2 cups flour
1 cup coconut
2 tsp baking powder
pinch of salt
chocolate icing and extra coconut for decoration

METHOD

Melt butter, sugar, cocoa and golden syrup in a large saucepan. Do not let it boil. Let it cool and then add flour, coconut, baking powder and salt.

Press into a greased and baking paper lined 22 x 30cm tin and bake at 180°C for 20 minutes only.

Remove from oven and leave for another 10 minutes and then ice with chocolate icing while still warm.

Sprinkle with extra coconut.

Cut into squares and store in an airtight tin.

✱ This is the most satisfying slice to make – dead easy and great tasting – but over the years I have perfected it and the results are most pleasing if you remove it from the oven right on 20 minutes, even if it looks a little uncooked, as that gives it a slightly fudgy consistency.

✱ Bear in mind it does not have eggs in it, and the better the cocoa, the better the results.

✱ Do line the dish with greased baking paper – it makes lifting out the iced slice so much easier.

✱ This slice was made in a regular bake oven – not fan-bake. If you only have fan-bake, then reduce the temperature by 10–20 degrees Celsius. After you have made it a few times, and know how your oven 'works', you can reduce that cooking temperature down to 170°C for 20 minutes if you prefer a slightly more moist result.

top a favourite chocolate cake with rich chocolate icing and fresh berries

BANANA CHOCOLATE CHIP MUFFINS

This recipe is ideal for you to use those sad overripe bananas sitting in your fruit bowl. These muffins are really more like small cakes and freeze well – they do not need icing or buttering. **Makes 16**

3 overripe bananas
125g soft butter
175g (about 3/4 cup) sugar
2 eggs
1 tblsp milk
1 tsp vanilla
175g (about 1 1/2 cups) self-raising flour
1 tsp baking soda
1 cup chocolate chips

METHOD

Blend the bananas in the food processor. Add the soft butter, sugar, eggs, milk and vanilla. Blend until smooth. Place the self-raising flour, soda and chocolate chips in a large bowl and gently add the banana mix to the dried ingredients. Stir gently until it is all well blended. Bake in large greased muffin pans at 180°C for 20 minutes.

February and the apricot season is eagerly awaited in my kitchen. Apricots are my terrible weakness. Sitting in a restaurant when the dessert menu is presented, I can pass on every dessert – except anything apricot. For me it's better than chocolate. An apricot crumble with a hint of coconut is deliciously wicked, a fresh apricot tart with contrasting intense flavours of zingy apricot combined with buttery pastry notes is simply a dream come true, and a slice of apricot dacquoise (a meringue with a hint of almonds layered with brandy cream and poached apricots all dusted with icing sugar) can send me into orbit.

THE APRICOT FILE

❋ Select apricots that are rich in colour with a delicate perfume. Ripen in a brown paper bag, away from direct sunlight.

❋ The 500g bag is perfect for making up a batch of jam. Wash, de-stone and cut into slices. Place in a pot with 1/4 cup water and a good squeeze of lemon juice. Heat gently, and when warmed add the sugar. Most jam recipes call for equal amounts of sugar to fruit. I never follow that rule, preferring to make small amounts of jam often and keeping the jam pot in the fridge. I usually add 375g of sugar to 500g of fruit. Cook gently and test jam for setting as per usual. It will never be as thick as regular jam, but the flavour is superb. Allow 15 minutes to make this jam.

❋ Add slices of fresh apricots to an apple crumble or apple pie. Make a favourite pound cake and add thin slices of fresh apricots. Top slices of cake with an apricot purée with a hint of brandy. Fresh apricots are also a full-flavoured addition to sweet muffins.

❋ Serve a delicious apricot and amaretto purée with slightly softened vanilla ice-cream. Place 500g halved and stoned apricots in a pan with 100g sugar. Add just enough water to cover the apricots. Bring to a boil, then reduce heat and simmer until just tender but still intact. Drain, reserve syrup and transfer to a bowl to cool. Place 1 cup cooked apricots in a blender and blend until smooth. Stir in 1 tblsp lemon juice. Boil reserved syrup until reduced by half and add 1–2 tblsp amaretto liqueur. Return apricots to syrup and leave at room temperature for a few hours until serving time. Serve the apricots with the purée over the ice-cream.

❋ Apricots and star anise partner well in a galette. Roll out flaky pastry to a 40cm circle – place on a lightly buttered oven tray and leave in the fridge for 30 minutes. Place 2 milk arrowroot biscuits, 1 tblsp sugar and 1 tblsp flour in a food processor and process until the mixture resembles breadcrumbs. Spread over the prepared pastry leaving a 6cm border. Gently toss 8–12 halved and stoned apricots in 1/3 cup sugar and place over pastry. Fold the uncovered border over the apricots, pleating it to fit. Scatter surface with 5–6 star anise. Bake at 175°C for 35 minutes or until golden. Rest 5 minutes before sliding onto a wire rack to cool for 5 minutes. Serve with ice-cream.

and plate, using a tea towel as the pan is hot, so the tart comes out easily onto the plate.

Serve warm with a scoop of vanilla ice-cream or cream.

* This Tarte Tatin is a variation on the classic upside-down apple pie created by the two French sisters by the name of Tatin. We have simplified it down to a process any home cook could manage with confidence, and while you traditionally use flaky pastry for a Tarte Tatin, you can use up a sheet of sweet short pastry (left over from Christmas mince pies), if you desire.

* The only non-negotiable feature is the cooking pan – you need a small frypan (cast iron works well) with an ovenproof handle that will easily transfer from the stove top to the oven and sustain the high heat.

LADY GLENORCHY'S NECTARINE TART

Lady Glenorchy, otherwise known as Deb Alley of Queenstown, is a very fine baker and no cookbook would be complete without one of her recipes. Use any stone fruit in this versatile tart.

1 sweet shortcrust pastry 23cm lined pie
 shell (place in freezer to keep cold)
2 tblsp apricot jam, plus extra jam reserved
 for glaze
fresh nectarines and strawberries
 and/or raspberries
2 tblsp flaked almonds

FILLING
120g unsalted butter, softened
150g (about 3/4 cup) caster sugar
200g (about 1½ cups) ground almonds
3 eggs
3 tblsp brandy (optional)

METHOD
Spread the pastry base with the apricot jam. To make the filling: blend the butter and sugar together, add the ground almonds, eggs and brandy (optional) and blend well. Spoon this mix into the uncooked pastry shell. Top with halves of fresh nectarines and berry fruit scattered in the gaps.

Bake at 180°C for 20 minutes, then reduce to 150°C for approximately 30 minutes or until the centre is springy to touch and the tart is golden in colour. Whilst hot, glaze with strained and heated apricot jam. Quickly toast the flaked almonds and sprinkle over the flan before serving.

Serve warm or cold, not hot. The almond flavour improves with a rest period and it is easier to cut.

* Warning: the aroma of the baking tart is simply divine and may encourage you to do something completely out of character!
* The pastry-lined pie plate kept in the freezer even for 15 minutes reduces shrinkage when baked.

APRICOT TARTE TATIN

Summer cooking should be this simple and totally irresistible.

100g butter
3 heaped tblsp brown sugar
8 apricots, stoned and sliced
1 sheet pre-rolled pastry (flaky or sweet short)
vanilla ice-cream or cream to serve

METHOD
Place the butter and brown sugar in a 22cm cast-iron frypan or other ovenproof pan. Heat gently, until you almost reach a caramel-looking syrup. Add the chopped apricots and cook gently until slightly softened, but still retaining their shape. Take off the heat and allow the bubbling syrup to subside.

Cut out a circle of pastry approximately 24cm wide and place over the fruit in the frypan and tuck under the sides, taking care as the fruit and syrup are burning hot. Bake in a 200°C fan bake oven for 15–20 minutes until golden. Leave to cool 5 minutes, then run a knife around the edge. Place a large white plate over the frypan and flip the pan

The honesty of a sun-ripened tomato is so appealing: cut in half, drizzle with a little good quality olive oil, season lightly with salt and pepper and escape to the garden with a piece of decent bread. Perfection.

You can top with fresh basil, add a slice of mozzarella cheese or slice of freshly roasted chicken, fresh salad greens, a dollop of pesto and the great flavours just keep evolving. Tomatoes can be enjoyed at all meals. Start the day with a tomato treat – try slices of fresh tomato on your wholemeal toast in the morning and you may never go back to the honey-pot.

The glut of cheap tomatoes at this time of the year is good news for the home cook. Tomatoes are so versatile, from soup to salsa, sauces to relish and chutney – tomato is the ubiquitous favourite. They are so inexpensive that you can afford to get adventurous and try something different. It's best to buy regular amounts of tomatoes as you need them.

So the bowl of tomatoes sits proudly on the bench and what do you do with them?

For fresh ideas, go from the simple – slice, season and alternate with slices of mozzarella cheese and top with a drizzle of pesto, or make bruschetta: firstly dice and season tomatoes with salt and pepper, drizzle with the extra virgin olive oil, a light splash of balsamic vinegar and some torn basil leaves and leave to sit at room temperature for a few hours. Place a spoonful on top of grilled sourdough bread slices that have been rubbed with garlic. If all this sounds too much – go for the freezer option. Simply cut your fresh tomatoes in half, sprinkle with a hint of sugar and season with salt and pepper. Place on a baking tray and roast for 1 hour at 150°C. Allow these tomato halves to cool and then freeze as per normal. This oven-roasting process ensures the frozen tomatoes are even more intensely flavoured and less watery when you use them later in soups, stews or pasta sauces. Perfect during the winter when bright summery days are a fleeting memory.

'The cherry tomato is a wonderful invention, producing, as it does, a satisfactorily explosive squish when bitten.'
MISS MANNERS (JUDITH MARTIN), AMERICAN COLUMNIST

TOMATO BITES

✳ Never ripen a tomato on the window-ledge — just put them in a bowl and don't refrigerate. Refrigeration kills the taste of tomatoes.

✳ To skin a tomato, cut a small cross in the bottom of the tomato and place in boiling water for 25 seconds. Remove and place in cold water, and when you can handle the heat of the tomato pull the skin away with a sharp knife.

✳ The experts say it is best to remove the skins and seeds from tomatoes before cooking. Seeds make a tomato sauce bitter when cooked. On an everyday level I don't bother — but if it for something special, then perhaps follow this rule.

✳ If you want to oven-dry your own tomatoes, place salted halves on cake racks and then on trays (lined with foil) in a 60°C oven for at least 8-10 hours — overnight is ideal.

✳ For a great classical tomato sauce to accompany seafood (even mussel fritters love the association), try filling a bowl with seasoned, diced fresh tomato. Add a splash of balsamic vinegar and freshly torn basil leaves and drizzle over slightly warmed extra virgin olive oil. Heat slightly but do not boil; the slight heat in the oil transforms this sauce — try it!

TOMATO BREAD (PA AMB TOMAQUET)

Ideally this recipe should be kept until the tomatoes are sitting plump on your vine in the late summer. This recipe toasts the bread and it is delicious, but in Spain I also enjoyed this with fresh bread.
Serves 4

8 thick slices sourdough bread
2 large garlic cloves, peeled and cut in
  half lengthwise
2 very ripe tomatoes, halved crosswise
2 tblsp olive oil
salt and freshly ground black pepper to taste

METHOD
Toast the bread on both sides. For garlic lovers, vigorously rub garlic, cut side down, on the warm toasted bread. Cupping a tomato half in your palm, rub 2 pieces of bread with it; squeeze the tomato so that not only the juice and seeds ooze into the bread, but also some pulp. Only the skin should be left.

Drizzle the olive oil over and sprinkle with salt and pepper to taste. This bread is best eaten straight away!

TOMATO, MINT & RED ONION SALAD

This delicious salad is so easy to make and the great news is that it does not call for fancy ingredients – between the back garden and the pantry you can whip this up without a trip to the supermarket. Make at least 30 minutes ahead of serving time and do not refrigerate. **Serves 4**

500g tomatoes
1/4 tsp sugar
1/4 tsp sea salt
1 tablespoon olive oil
1 tsp red wine vinegar
8 fresh mint leaves, thinly sliced
1 small red onion, thinly sliced
freshly ground black pepper

METHOD

Cut the tomatoes into 6mm thick slices and arrange half the slices in one layer in a shallow serving dish. In a small bowl combine the sugar and the salt and sprinkle the layer of tomatoes with half the mixture. Arrange the remaining tomato slices on top and sprinkle them with the remaining sugar mixture. Drizzle the tomatoes with oil and the vinegar and let the salad stand at room temperature for 30 minutes. Sprinkle the salad with mint and arrange the onion, drained and separated into rings, on top. Finally, season with freshly ground black pepper.

> 'Summer cooking implies a sense of immediacy, a capacity to capture the essence of the fleeting moment.'
> ELIZABETH DAVID

Never have a few words so well described the plum season. Right on cue, the backyard plum tree is laden with fruit and you have a day or two before the birds beat you to it. Desperation sets in for home cooks. Too busy with the great weather to make jam and sauce, the plums are quickly stuffed into freezer bags and marked for later use. Friends and family arrive for coffee and leave laden with red, pert, plump stone fruit.

Plums in New Zealand are vastly underrated – in parts of Europe the plum season is so celebrated that cakes, pastries and tarts suddenly appear with a fanfare completely dedicated to and glistening with fresh plum slices. The results are deliciously sublime. They often add a little hazelnut or almond into the equation and achieve a culinary masterpiece.

Even if you pick up a bag of plums at the fruit market for $2 – take them home and get busy: plums will reward you with much versatility and flavour enhancement. Everyone loves home-made plum jam, and plum sauce is perfect with those barbecued sausages.

But to really enjoy plums in their purest, simplest form, try this sublime dessert. Wash plums, cut in half, de-stone and place on a baking tray with sides and lined with foil. Have the cavity side facing upwards. Sprinkle with a little brandy (brandy loves all fruit with a stone), then a light dusting of raw or brown sugar and grill or barbecue until lightly coloured, but still in shape. The sugar caramelises the intense fruit flavour and the whole process will only take a few minutes. Serve with natural yoghurt combined with your favourite liquid honey, or crème fraîche combined with passionfruit syrup (add a squeeze of orange juice) and a platter of home-made biscuits.

HAZELNUT PLUM CAKE

3 tblsp butter
1 tsp vanilla
1/2 cup whole hazelnuts or whole almonds (about 70g)
1/2 cup brown sugar
1/3 cup flour
3 large egg whites
1/4 tsp salt
2 medium plums (about 250g), thinly sliced
11/2 tsp sugar
icing sugar for sifting over cake
vanilla ice-cream to serve

METHOD
Preheat oven to 220°C. Butter and flour a 20cm round cake pan, knocking out excess flour.

In a small saucepan melt butter over moderate heat and cool. Stir in vanilla. In a food processor blend together nuts, brown sugar and flour until nuts are finely ground.

In a bowl with an electric mixer beat whites with salt until they hold stiff peaks, then fold in nut mixture gently

but thoroughly. Fold in butter mixture (batter will deflate) and spread batter in prepared pan.

Arrange plum slices evenly over batter and sprinkle with sugar. Bake cake in middle of oven for 20–25 minutes, or until a tester comes out clean. Turn cake out onto rack and cool, plum side up, for 5 minutes.

To serve, sift icing sugar over the cooled cake.

THE PLUM FILE

* If you are feeling lazy but want to make a great simple plum dessert cake – place 1 1/4 cups self-raising flour in a bowl (or plain flour with a heaped tsp baking powder) with 3/4 cup sugar and blend together. Add 120g melted butter and 2 eggs and a drop or two of vanilla essence. Pour into a greased 24cm loose-bottomed cake tin. Top with 4 cups sliced plums (skin on, stone out). Add a few berries (whatever is left over from Christmas) or 1 or 2 sliced apricots for contrast, and push down on the mix, then sprinkle with 2-3 tblsp sugar and bake at 180°C for 1 hour.

* Plums make a great partner in a salad with roasted beetroot and goat cheese. Roast beetroot and drizzle with a favourite walnut oil vinaigrette with a hint of sugar. Serve with fresh spinach leaves and slices of fresh plums and crumble goat cheese over the top.

* Pickle plums – delicious with cold meat and cheese platters. Bring 600ml white wine vinegar, 12 black peppercorns, 1 tsp whole cloves, 4 cardamom pods, 2 cinnamon sticks and 2 star anise to a boil. Add 1kg sugar and boil gently for 2 minutes. Add 2kg dark red, halved plums and simmer for 4–5 minutes. Bottle, but do not seal. Keep in the fridge.

* If you want to try a simple plum rustic tart, roll out your favourite flaky pastry into a circle on a greased baking sheet and fill with 500g plums, halved and pitted. Cut plums into 2cm-thick wedges and in a bowl toss with 1/2 cup sugar, 1 1/2 tblsp cornflour, and 2 tblsp lemon juice. Place in centre of pastry circle with pastry left around the circle to place over the fruit. Pull up sides around the fruit – do not worry if there is a gap in the centre as rustic means non-fussy and the circle of exposed fruit in the centre is desirable. Bake pie in middle of 190°C oven for 45 minutes. Brush crust with milk and sprinkle with sugar. Bake pie 10 minutes more, or until filling is bubbling and crust is golden. Cool pie on a rack.

* Make a plum crisp. In a bowl stir together 4–5 cups sliced plums, 2 tsp lemon juice, and 1/4–1/2 cup sugar, then spread the mixture evenly in the bottom of a buttered baking dish. In another bowl blend 1/3 cup brown sugar, 1/3 cup flour, 1/2 cup rolled oats, 1 tsp cinnamon, 1/2 tsp ginger, 1/4 cup chopped walnuts and 3 tblsp cold butter until the mixture resembles coarse meal. Sprinkle the brown sugar mixture evenly over the plum mixture and bake the dessert for 30–35 minutes in the middle of a preheated oven at 190°C, or until it is crisp. Serve the plum crisp warm with vanilla ice-cream. Serves 2 plum enthusiasts.

* Make a great plum salsa for your next roast chicken salsa. In a bowl stir together 3 cups sliced plums with 1/3 cup minced red onion, 1/2 cup chopped coriander, 1/4 cup chopped mint, 1/2–1 tsp minced chilli (jalapeno is ideal), 1 tblsp lime juice, 1 tsp sugar, and salt and pepper to taste.

* Make a super, simple plum and raspberry compote. Combine 1kg sliced plums and 2 punnets raspberries in a large bowl. Combine 1 bottle 750ml dry red wine (Beaujolais is ideal), 1 1/2 cups water and 1 cup sugar in a large saucepan. Scrape in seeds from 1 split vanilla bean, then add bean. Stir over medium heat until sugar dissolves. Increase heat and boil until reduced to 2 2/3 cups, about 20 minutes. Pour hot wine mixture over plum mixture. Cool. Cover and chill overnight. Spoon fruit mixture into dessert glasses or bowls. Top with whipped cream.

GINGER PLUM BARBECUE SAUCE

500g red plums, cut into 2.5cm chunks
1 tblsp finely grated peeled fresh ginger
2 garlic cloves, chopped
4 tblsp hoisin sauce
2 tblsp brown sugar
2 tblsp water
1 tblsp soy sauce
2 star anise
1 tblsp cider vinegar
2 spring onions, chopped

METHOD
In a covered saucepan simmer all ingredients except vinegar and spring onions, stirring occasionally, until plums are falling apart – about 20 minutes. Add vinegar and simmer, uncovered, stirring frequently, until sauce is consistency of tomato sauce – about 10 minutes. Discard star anise and stir in spring onions. Keep in a sealed container in the fridge. Delicious with roast or barbecued chicken, pork, and transforms a simple sausage. Makes about 1 cup sauce.

TRADITIONAL PLUM SAUCE

2.75kg plums
1.8kg sugar
2 cups malt vinegar
4 onions, chopped
2 tsp ground cloves
2 tsp black pepper
1 1/2 tblsp ground ginger
2 level tblsp salt

METHOD
Cut the plums in half and place in a large stockpot with all the other ingredients. Boil for 2 1/2–3 hours until mixture thickens, stirring from time to time. Pass through a sieve to remove stones and pour into hot glass bottles.

* If you remove the stones from the fruit before cooking, then you do not have to sieve it before placing in bottles. Don't worry if a stone does find its way into the finished product – my Granny always made this sauce and in later years used to say the odd stone added flavour!

MARCH in Belgium

March, and my destination was Brussels. Belgium does not figure highly on gastronomic tours of Europe, more is the pity. Sure, most cooks know about the mussels and frites with mayonnaise, the heavenly chocolates, the waffles, the beer, the delightful Bruges for a day trip, but is there more?

For me, Belgium has always been a delight to visit, so any trip to London or Europe must always include a trip to Brussels. Sometimes I make the most ridiculous diversions to get back to Hotel Pacific in Brussels, just a few minutes' walk from the Grand Place, the main square in the centre of town. The attraction is the patron/owner Paul Pauwels – a warm, engaging, sympathetic man who helps you with your luggage, answers all your questions, heats up the furnace at the prescribed hour for you to have a quick shower, organises a tea tray with special bread and restorative tea on arrival and fills you with wonderful, colourful stories about his relatives who were explorers in the Belgian Congo. The shower is on the first floor, and you may be on the fourth floor, the small lift creaks with your luggage and the beds and linen remind you of your grandmother's house.

Paul is unique. It's not often that you write the word 'kind' and 'caring' about someone who has been operating a hotel for fifteen years, but this 70-plus patron gets up 7 days a week at 6.30 a.m., 365 days a year, to collect great bread and make omelettes to serve with cheese for hungry travellers. (The secret to his omelettes, he says, is a little milk, fast heat and beating the eggs until frothy, so plenty of air gets into the mix.) It's a great breakfast. Divine hot chocolate, tea or coffee, the best bread, cheese and ham, jams and that memorable omelette.

On my first trip to Europe this was my first hotel and my first taste of anything Continental. The bread had me in a highly excited state – Paul teasingly gave me the label 'beaucoup de manger', which literally means 'much appetite or eating'. If you visit, tell him 'beaucoup de manger' sent you and he will order more bread and you will be very grateful indeed.

All in all a very simple hotel, full of backpackers and those of us 'retired backpackers' who keep going back because we just love Paul so much.

CARBONADE A LA FLAMANDE

Another classic Belgian dish – always make this ahead and reheat the next day for great flavours.

1kg diced beef
seasoned flour for coating
2 onions, sliced
6 cloves garlic, crushed
1/2 cup pitted prunes
2 bay leaves
2 tsp thyme
1–2 tblsp Dijon mustard
300ml dark beer
300ml beef stock
2 slices stale bread, crumbled

METHOD

Season the flour with salt and pepper, toss the beef in the flour and sauté a few pieces at a time in hot oil for a few minutes until the meat has sealed well. Place in a casserole dish.

Add the onion and garlic to the hot oil and cook until translucent and soft and add to the casserole, along with the rest of the ingredients.

Add a few slices of crumbled up stale bread to thicken the stew. Bake in a 160°C oven for 2 hours, covered.

✱ Long, slow cooking is ideal for this recipe. Serve with mashed potatoes and other vegetables.

CELERY ONION MUSSELS

Try this simple Belgium-inspired treatment of local mussels.

100ml dry white wine
1/2 cup finely sliced onion
1/2 cup finely sliced celery
2 cloves garlic, crushed
1 tsp fresh thyme
a bay leaf
4 sprigs parsley, chopped
1kg mussels, with beards removed

METHOD

Bring the wine to the boil and add the rest of the ingredients. Add the mussels and cover the pot and give it a shake/swirl to mix up the ingredients. Simmer until the mussels open. Discard any mussels that do not open.

APRIL in France ... to live in a small village and to cook fresh seasonal produce

✱ Belgium is the area for steaming pots of savoury, small, black-lipped mussels, piles of fresh cream chocolates, elegant and crisp frites with mayonnaise, potato, meat and vegetable stews, beef braised tenderly in beer, waffles, great coffee and witlof.

✱ Sitting in the Hotel Pacific dining room you can feel the history of this small hotel. It was once a café for the workers from the nearby fish markets and got its name during the Second World War when Canadian and other Allied troops would meet at the hotel/café and nicknamed it Hotel Pacific.

The dining room today is reminiscent of a café from last century. Paul's family has been operating this hotel for generations. Memorabilia is scattered on the walls, and his stories and breadth of knowledge inspires and delights.

Ask for a direction and the teacher's pointer comes out and the large map near the stairs is quickly referred to. After 15 years (since my first visit) Paul remembers the room I had last time and tells me his main dream in life is to sail on Auckland harbour.

Hotel Pacific, 57 rue Antoine Dansaert, Brussels, ph. 02 511 84 59. No credit cards. A single room with breakfast is just under NZ$50 and a double about NZ$75.

✱ Le Roy D' Espagne, 1 Grand Place – a favourite café on the Grand Place. Atmospheric and good coffee. Expect to pay about NZ$4.50 for a coffee and small biscuit. Warning: they charge you to use the rest-rooms – otherwise a delightful experience. Ph. 02 513 08 07.

✱ Chez Leon, 18–20 rue des Bouchers, just off the Grand Place. Open daily noon–midnight. At first glance you may dismiss this as a tourist trap, but this institution has been churning out good meals since 1893 and is great for moules and frites (mussels and fries). Accepts credit cards. Ph. 02 511 14 15. Dinner and beer for 3, NZ$100.

✱ Café du Roy restaurant, 14 Grand Place. Climb down some stairs from the delightful Grand Place and enjoy some superb traditional Belgian food. Delicious soup and full-flavoured beef cooked slowly in beer. A three-course menu for NZ$35. Ph. 02 502 14 11.

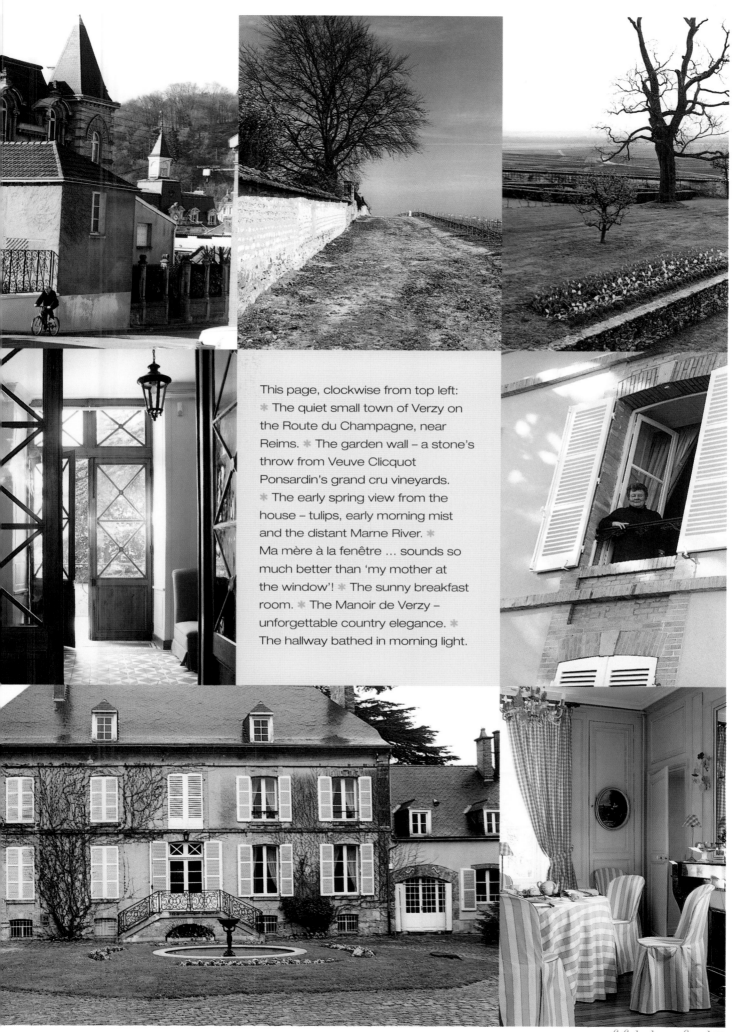

This page, clockwise from top left:
* The quiet small town of Verzy on the Route du Champagne, near Reims. * The garden wall – a stone's throw from Veuve Clicquot Ponsardin's grand cru vineyards. * The early spring view from the house – tulips, early morning mist and the distant Marne River. * Ma mère à la fenêtre … sounds so much better than 'my mother at the window'! * The sunny breakfast room. * The Manoir de Verzy – unforgettable country elegance. * The hallway bathed in morning light.

Ever since I had French lessons with Sister Basil at the age of 11, I have been fascinated with every aspect of the French way of life. Images of men with berets on their heads, riding bikes with strings of garlic or onions around their necks and baguettes in their baskets are all mixed with pictures of stylish women wearing glamorous sunglasses and Chanel suits, the glorious buildings and monuments in Paris, and that smoky café on the Left Bank. For most of us it is the most romantic and desirable destination possible.

To go to France for a month and live in a village was the ideal. Not in the high season with the tourists and not in Provence, but in a real working village where the local Tabac did not sell postcards. The luxury of travelling, you could tell people, without having to constantly move around.

My dream became a reality: a sojourn in Verzy, a tiny village on the Route du Champagne, living in Madame Clicquot's former country home. The village was incredibly quiet, shutters closed over windows every day, and the experience was both restorative and rewarding. Today, whenever I hear the sound of church bells, smell the perfume of lilacs, hear the soft cooing of doves or detect the unmistakable aroma of French bread being baked in a wood-fired oven, I'm transported back to this little village. Every exchange in every store selling vegetables to bread to meats was protracted and elaborate, from greetings to the shopkeeper, acknowledging all the other customers, and the ensuing animated discussion about one's health and the weather – the simplest transaction could take hours.

The highlight of the week was the Saturday morning market in Reims, where the plump, perfect, ash-covered goats' cheeses sat proudly beside artisan breads, piles of white asparagus glistened in the early morning sun, and salad greens looked fresh, varied and inviting. Stacks of wild mushrooms, small posies of lily of the valley picked from the forest, and tartes and cakes resplendent with their topping of fresh wild strawberries or honey-drenched apples completed just one end of this popular market.

Food producers and farmers wearing navy utilitarian coats or overalls with their berets or small cloth caps sat attentively beside their produce, happy to debate the merits of their wares and eager to banter – lively and welcoming stuff.

Every morning the chorus of pigeons woke us up and the bells from the church next to the house resounded with great deafening clarity. Every night my joy was to work with the large industrial gas stove in the kitchen.

Here I roasted chickens, cooked fish, made omelettes and prepared seasonal vegetables. Asparagus, potatoes, delicious vine-ripened tomatoes, glorious cheeses, sausage and pristine salad ingredients were all part of the evolving menu. It was the most magical time, and each morning I would check the progress on the vines below the house.

The food was superb, the chance to become absorbed by the village quite enchanting, and a firm, lifetime fondness for any Veuve Clicquot product is assured. I kept watch, you see, from my room overlooking the grapes. It's important, I'm sure you will agree, for a girl to see the process through to its deliciously, liquid completion!

TUNA NIÇOISE SALAD
This is a classic French salad. Enjoy for lunch with a glass of wine and a basket of bread!
Serves 4

450g can tuna
salt and freshly ground black pepper to taste
300g fresh green beans, blanched and refreshed
500g baby potatoes, halved and steamed
4–6 tomatoes, cut into wedges
1/3 telegraph cucumber, thinly sliced
6 hard-boiled eggs, quartered
12 anchovies
1/2 cup olives

LEMON JUICE DRESSING
juice of 2 lemons
1/3 cup extra virgin olive oil
salt and freshly ground black pepper

METHOD
Drain the tuna. Combine all the salad ingredients together except for the tuna, eggs and anchovies. Make the dressing by whisking lemon juice and oil together and seasoning with salt and pepper.

Drizzle the dressing over the salad and lightly toss through (reserving some for tuna).

Place on individual serving plates. Top salad with tuna and drizzle with remaining dressing. Season. Garnish with eggs and anchovies.

✳ You can add feta or mozzarella to this salad if desired, but this is not traditional.
✳ You can use fresh tuna, but remember to cook your fresh tuna steaks rare to medium rare or the tuna will be tough. Sear on a hot plate and then leave to rest.

THE FRENCH FILE

✳ Forget haute cuisine in France with its rich, unctuous cream sauces, fussy timbales, contrived little aspic numbers, fancy mousses and orchestrated plates and platters. No, the best food in France is peasant food, the food of the home and hearth, what Grandma used to make and which is now found, if you are lucky, in a simple bistro or family-run restaurant in a small village or country lane. This may sound far-fetched, romantic and unattainable, but fear not, even with a low New Zealand dollar you can still eat well-prepared meals in simple eateries. Select the carte du jour or menu of the day and you can pay as little as NZ$25 a head for a three- to four-course meal, and a glass of wine or cup of coffee may be thrown in as well. Just ask locally about good simple food and follow the crowds – good places are popular.

✳ French soup – we always think of French onion soup, but also try a delicious country-style vegetable soup. Into a large pot sweat onion, garlic and a little chopped bacon in a generous knob of butter. When the onion has softened, add diced potato and other root vegetables. Stir well, then cover the vegetables generously with milk; do not boil, just simmer until the vegetables are soft. Add chopped raw spinach and soften. Purée soup with a kitchen whiz and season with salt and pepper and chopped parsley. You can add a pinch of curry to the vegetables cooking in the butter, if desired, but the French style is to just celebrate the delicious, unadulterated vegetable flavours.

✳ Showcase roast chicken – the French have made rotisserie chicken an art form. They are superb! Find a delicious organic, free-range bird, squeeze lemon juice inside the cavity and stuff with stuffing or leave the lemon inside the cavity. Season well and insert plenty of herbs under the skin, on top and under the bird itself. Delicious with mashed potatoes or roast vegetables or simply salad.

✳ Serve cheese as a course – the French are so serious about cheese that it is rumoured a French man will not propose marriage to a woman who cannot tell if a Camembert is ripe or not! Get the cheese out of the fridge and let it come up to room temperature before serving. Have no more than three wedges of different cheese and serve with toast or crackers. The French serve cheese on a plate with a knife and fork – nothing else – but if you enjoy fruit, why not have a centre piece of grapes and a bowl of perfectly ripe pears so everyone can mix and mingle.

✳ Think braises and covered, slow cooking – invest in a Dutch covered casserole dish to make Coq au Vin and other delicious long and slow cooking recipes.

✳ French restaurants serve delicious country-style salads at lunch – try cubes of Gruyère cheese and ham combined with grated carrots, tomatoes and spring onions, dressed with a herb vinaigrette made with a spoonful of wholegrain mustard. A squeeze of orange juice into the salad dressing will give it extra freshness, and the sweet citrus flavour marries well with the oil and mustard.

✳ Another French salad option that is simply delicious – serve warm goats' cheese over tossed salad greens and with a basket of French bread.

✳ Have a French breakfast this weekend – strong coffee, warm croissants or slices of good French bread, jams and a pottle of yoghurt. The French lead the world in yoghurt consumption, so don't forget that addition. Any leftovers of croissants or French bread make a great bread and butter pudding.

✳ Make soups and chowders and serve with fresh bread – keep the portions generous and enjoy for days afterwards.

✳ Make a simple Coq au Vin. Toss chicken thighs in seasoned flour (dried herbs, salt and pepper), cook in a pan with olive oil until lightly golden and place in a Dutch oven or casserole. You can then fast track and add your favourite vegetables (carrot, mushrooms, celery, onion, etc), and chopped bacon and garlic on top of the chicken. Slosh in a little red wine, add a handful of chopped herbs and pour a jar of pasta sauce or canned tomatoes over the lot, cover and cook at 180°C (no more) for 1 hour.

GREEN BEANS WITH LIME AND ALMOND VINAIGRETTE

The secret to this side dish is to ensure you do not overcook the beans – they should be bright in colour and quite firm to bite. Search out a serious bean supplier near you! This recipe comes from top Auckland chef Geoff Scott, a confirmed Francophile. Serves 6

juice of 2 limes
100ml virgin olive oil
1/2 tsp Dijon mustard
2 tblsp coarsely
  chopped parsley
salt and freshly ground
  black pepper
100g whole peeled almonds
500g fresh dwarf or
  runner beans

METHOD
Mix the first six ingredients together well or shake vigorously in a jar with a tight lid. Place the almonds on a tray and bake in a 150°C oven until lightly golden.

Top and tail your beans and boil them in a large pot of salted water or steam them in a steamer. Do not overcook. Drain and toss immediately in the vinaigrette.

Scatter the roasted almonds over the top and decorate with sliced limes.

A SIMPLE FRENCH BEEF STEW

This ever-popular beef stew is a savoury delight –
a great idea for family dining. Make ahead as
the flavours improve with age, and never rush
the process – it just doesn't work! **Serves 4–6**

olive oil/butter for sautéing
3–4 rashers bacon, chopped
1kg beef steak (skirt or cross-cut blade), cubed
3 tblsp flour
1/2 tsp freshly ground black pepper
sea salt
1 bay leaf
2 tsp fresh basil or 1/2 tsp dried
2 cloves garlic, crushed
1 tsp dried oregano
2 cups beef stock
1 cup red wine
2 tblsp tomato paste
pinch of sugar
1 large onion, chopped
2–4 carrots
salt and freshly ground black pepper
freshly chopped parsley and herbs

METHOD

Heat olive oil in a frypan, add bacon and meat and brown
beef well on all sides. Take care not to place too much
meat in the frypan at once or it will 'stew' rather than brown.

Once browned on all sides, place beef/bacon in a
casserole.

Add a little more oil and butter to the pan. Add the flour,
seasoning and herbs to the pan, taking care to scrape all
the bits off the bottom. Once the flour is lightly coloured,
add the stock, wine, tomato paste and pinch of sugar to
de-glaze the pan. Allow to cook out and thicken, then
pour over the beef in the casserole. Cover and cook in
the oven for 3 hours at 150°C.

Melt another knob of butter in the frypan and cook the
onion and carrots until lightly coloured, then add to
casserole after 1 hour of cooking.

Season with salt and freshly ground black pepper.

* You can add other vegetables such as
mushrooms, parsnips, potatoes and kumara if
desired. If your stew is not as thick as you desire,
when it is completely cooked just blend 2 tblsp soft
butter with 2 tblsp flour and add to the hot stew.
It will thicken and add gloss to the stew.

* Serve the stew in a bowl with a basket of bread
to mop up the gravy. Sprinkle each bowl of stew with
chopped parsley and other fresh herbs.

Many years ago, my cousin Graeme went to live in a village in France in the Auvergne region, in the heart of the Massif Central, a mountain range with a chain of long-extinct volcanoes, known locally as 'Puy'. He taught English over eight summers, perfected his impressive knowledge of the local language and developed a serious love affair with the local Puy lentils. To this day, he quietly corrects the pronunciation of the word Puy. If you're not in the know, you pronounce Puy like 'we' but with a 'p'. Now this may sound pretentious, but my cousin is not a culinary snob – he's just infatuated with the simplicity, flavour and integrity of the green Puy lentil.

The Puy lentil is prized around the world for its delicate, peppery flavour and ability to keep shape after strenuous cooking. This unique flavour comes from the dry climate and volcanic soil in this region. Like other legumes, lentils are low in fat and high in protein and fibre, but they have the added advantage of cooking quickly. Lentils have a mild, often earthy flavour, and they are best if cooked with assertive flavourings. Puy lentils work well with goats' cheese, wild boar, duck and salted pork, yet also happily accompany braised lamb, a chargrilled piece of fresh salmon or roasted lemon chicken. Puy lentils take longer to cook than other lentils. The milder brown lentils also hold their shape after cooking, but can easily turn mushy if overcooked. Indian markets also carry a wide variety of split lentils called dhal. Before cooking brown lentils, always rinse lentils and pick out stones and other debris. Unlike dried beans and peas, there's no need to soak them. Lentils cook more slowly if they're combined with salt or acidic ingredients, so add these last. Bigger or older lentils take longer to cook. Store dried lentils for up to a year in a cool dry place.

To show my Francophile cousin true affection, I invite him over for dinner or lunch and serve him Puy lentil salad. With a dramatic flourish, a huge bowl is placed in front of him at the table. Leftovers are boxed up and sent home. He says these are his favourite – cooked slowly with good quality chicken stock, salt added at the end, drizzled with a gutsy vinaigrette and combined with diced tomato, fresh herbs, feta or cooked smoked bacon, peppers or artichokes. A meal in itself! Serve at room temperature, with just a little warmth left to the salad. The flavours are simply sensational.

LENTIL SALAD WITH TOMATOES AND FETA

Another variation on the Puy lentil salad theme – the feta cheese and fresh tomato bring strong flavour and a zingy freshness to the French classic cupboard staple.
Serves 6

1 cup Puy lentils
2 tblsp red wine vinegar
1 shallot, minced
1 tblsp Dijon mustard
1/4 cup extra virgin olive oil
salt and freshly ground
 black pepper
1 1/3 cups diced, seeded,
 peeled cucumber
2/3 cup diced,
 seeded tomatoes
1/3 cup finely chopped
 red onion
2 tblsp chopped fresh dill
3–4 tblsp chopped
 fresh parsley
2 large cloves garlic, minced
200g crumbled feta
 or soft fresh goat cheese

METHOD
Cook lentils in medium pot of boiling, lightly salted water until just tender, about 25 minutes. Drain well.

Combine vinegar, shallot and mustard in large bowl. Gradually whisk in oil. Season with salt and pepper. Add lentils. Let stand until cool.

Add cucumber, tomatoes, onion, dill, parsley and garlic to lentils. Season with salt and pepper. Cover; chill for 1 hour.

Scatter feta or goats' cheese over salad and mix gently to combine.

GRAEME'S WARM PUY LENTIL SALAD
Serves 4–6

500g (1 packet) Sabarot
 Puy lentils
chicken stock and water
 to cover lentils
1 whole onion, peeled and
 stuck with two cloves
a bouquet garni (bay leaf,
 thyme and parsley)
3–4 peppercorns
1 small carrot, diced
1 packet capocollo (dry-cured
 and air-dried pork) or 200g
 cooked bacon, diced
1 large ripe tomato, diced
280g jar artichokes, drained
200g jar Spanish peppers,
 drained
chopped parsley to garnish

METHOD
Cook the lentils in the chicken stock
(just cover the lentils with stock).
Bring to the boil and add onion, herbs,
peppercorns and carrot. Cover and
simmer gently for 45–60 minutes.
The cooking time will vary slightly –
but you want them still firm not mushy.

Sauté the bacon or grill the capocollo
and make the vinaigrette.

Drain the lentils, place in a bowl and
remove onion and bouquet garni and
peppercorns. Add the bacon, diced
tomato, artichokes and Spanish
peppers. Drizzle with vinaigrette
and sprinkle with parsley. (pictured page 26)

VINAIGRETTE

100ml extra virgin olive oil
50ml chardonnay vinegar
1–2 cloves garlic, crushed
squeeze of lemon juice
salt if needed

✳ Delicious on its own, this salad
is divine with chargrilled salmon
(coat with brown sugar, rice wine
vinegar, soy sauce, sesame oil
and Dijon mustard) and mashed
potatoes.

✳ If you do not have the artichokes
or the Spanish peppers, do not
worry – they add great flavour and
variety to the salad, but without
them the salad is equally delicious!

SERVING SUGGESTIONS

✳ The simplest way to cook
lentils is to cook 500g lentils,
3 cloves garlic and 2 sprigs
of thyme in boiling salted water
for 25 minutes or until lentils
are just tender. Drain and
discard thyme; reserve garlic.
Heat 40g butter in same
saucepan, add 2 ripe, peeled
and diced tomatoes and chopped
reserved garlic and cook for 1
minute. Add lentils, season well
with salt, and stir until heated
through. Remove lentils from
heat and stir some chopped
parsley through. Perfect with
braised meats.

✳ Combine bulgur with Puy
lentils and a hint of tarragon
and some chopped walnuts for
a great textured salad. Take
1/3 cup finely chopped shallot
and let it rest with 3 tblsp
tarragon wine vinegar. Cook
1/2 cup Puy lentils. When cooked
and softened, add hot lentils
to shallot mixture and season
with salt and pepper. Cool
mixture, stirring occasionally.
In a small saucepan combine
11/2 cups water, 1 cup bulgur
and salt to taste and simmer,
covered, until water is absorbed
(allow 12 to 15 minutes).
Transfer bulgur to a large bowl
and cool completely, stirring
occasionally. Add lentils to
bulgur with 1/2 cup finely
chopped celery, 1/2 cup grated
carrot, 3 tblsp fresh tarragon,
2 tblsp vinegar, 3 tblsp extra
virgin olive oil, 1/2 cup
chopped walnuts, and salt and
pepper to taste; toss well.
Salad may be made 1 day ahead
and chilled, covered. Bring
salad to room temperature
before serving.

✳ Top Australian chef Philippe
Mouchel's Lentil Salad is used
to smartly garnish braised offal
such as pig's trotters, and is
in itself a much-requested dish.
To make the lentil salad, blanch
400g lentils in water and then
rinse. In fresh water bring
rinsed lentils, 1/2 an onion,
some cloves, 1 chopped carrot
and 1 small bouquet garni to
the boil and simmer until
lentils are cooked. (A bouquet
garni is traditionally a very
small tied bundle of bay leaf,
thyme and parsley.) For the
dressing, bring 200ml white
wine vinegar, 2 sprigs rosemary
and 2 tsp orange zest to the
boil, then take off heat. Once
cooled, add 4 cloves crushed
garlic, 600ml olive oil and
salt and pepper. Strain dressing
and toss through warm lentils.

✳ Make a simple Puy lentil and
couscous salad. Cook lentils,
and when drained add 1 tblsp
vinegar. Prepare couscous
(using instructions on packet)
and add a little oil as you
fluff grains with a fork. In
a small bowl whisk together
1 crushed large garlic clove
minced with a little salt,
2 tblsp vinegar, 3 tblsp oil,
and salt and pepper to taste.
Stir lentils and dressing into
couscous. Chill salad, covered,
for at least 3 hours, or up
to twenty-four. Just before
serving, stir in 1/2 cup finely
chopped fresh mint leaves, 1
bunch rocket (stems discarded
and leaves washed well, spun
dry, and chopped), 2 cups
vine-ripened cherry tomatoes,
halved, and 125g feta, crumbled
(about 1 cup). Season with
salt (if needed) and pepper.

✳ Make Puy lentil soup. Bring
6 cups water to a boil in a
stockpot. Add 250g lentils, 1
large chopped onion, 4 celery
sticks, a handful of garden
herbs, 1 bay leaf, 2-3 cloves
garlic, 1 tsp English mustard
and black pepper. Boil rapidly
for 15 minutes until frothy.
Remove froth with a spoon and
discard. Reduce heat and simmer
for 2 hours until smooth. Put
in blender for a smoother soup.
Add salt. Serve red hot with
buttered grainy rolls.

✳ Puy lentils are available in
good delis and food stores and
in some gourmet sections of the
supermarket.

MAY ... the autumn table

Autumn with crisper days, softer sunlight and longer shadows encourages the home cook indoors. The harvest table is literally groaning with produce: fresh mushrooms, pert apples, sensual pears, the last of the glossy capsicums, new kumara and pumpkins, aromatic quinces and the last of the passionfruit.

Make an excuse to celebrate the best of what's available now. Take some passionfruit, for example, and make a favourite sour cream cake. Cream 125g softened butter with 1 cup sugar, add 3 lightly beaten eggs and fold in 1 cup flour with 1 tsp baking powder alternately with 1/2 cup light sour cream. Fold in the pulp of 1–2 passionfruit and bake in a 20cm cake tin at 160°C for 45–55 minutes. While still warm drizzle the cake with passionfruit pulp. See bottom picture on Contents page for inspiration.

HONEYED FIGS

Autumn is a delightful time of year. Crisp mornings, bright blue skies, but the intensity and humidity of the summer days has long since passed. It's time to pick figs and other autumnal fruits and get excited about apples again!

6 whole ripe figs
1 tblsp liquid honey
1 tblsp butter
pinch of salt

METHOD
Wash and gently dry figs. Place in a small ovenproof dish. Melt honey and butter together and pour over figs, then sprinkle with salt.

 Serve with duck or chicken. Just roast with either for the last 15–20 minutes. Spoon honey and butter mix over figs from time to time while roasting .

FUNKY PUMPKIN SOUP

This is a simple traditional pumpkin soup recipe without any milk or cream, except for a garnish and that is optional. You can remove the curry and the ginger if you prefer plain flavours. After making the soup, if the pumpkin flavour needs extra vibrancy, add a squeeze of fresh lemon or lime juice to the pot – lifts the whole soup up on flavour!

knob of butter and a little olive oil
1 onion, chopped
3–4 cloves garlic, minced
1 tsp grated fresh ginger
2 tblsp mild curry paste
3–4 rashers bacon, rind removed and chopped
1/2 cup buttercup pumpkin pieces, peeled and seeded
5 cups chicken stock or 4 cups stock and 1 water
light seasoning of salt and freshly ground black pepper
coconut cream to garnish
fresh herbs such as coriander or thyme for garnish

METHOD
Place the butter and oil in a large stockpot. Add onion, garlic and ginger and cook until softened on a gentle heat. Add curry paste and when fragrant (allow just 30–60 seconds) add chopped bacon and pumpkin pieces.

Constantly turn the pumpkin in the paste/bacon mixture to avoid catching – this is an important stage for flavour enhancement. Add the stock or stock and water and cook until the pumpkin has softened, and then process with a kitchen whizz. Season and garnish with coconut cream and fresh herbs.

PUMPKIN SOUP BITES

✳ Better made a day ahead of serving

✳ Serve with a basket of bread.

✳ The reason for the combination of butter and oil at the beginning of the soup is that butter gives great flavour - but oil increases the 'flash point' in other words, behaves better when heated!

✳ Remember the soup will only be as good as the stock.

great weekend eating ...

POTATO-CRUSTED QUICHE

This quiche is great for brunch as well as for dinner – just serve with a mixed green salad and some crusty bread. The aged Cheddar gives this pie a wonderful flavour! **Serves 4–6**

olive oil spray
4 medium potatoes, peeled and thinly sliced
1 tblsp olive oil
1 cup chopped onion
1 cup chopped capsicum
2 tsp fresh thyme
1 cup diced bacon
8 large eggs
1/4 tsp salt
1/2 tsp black pepper
1 cup grated mature Cheddar cheese

METHOD

Preheat the oven to 180°C. Spray a pie dish with olive oil spray. Line the prepared pie dish with the potato rounds, overlapping slightly. Cover and microwave until tender. Allow to cool.

Heat olive oil in a frypan and add onion, capsicum and thyme and slowly sauté for 5 minutes. Add bacon and cook 1 more minute. Spoon over potatoes in pie dish. Whisk eggs together in a large bowl with the salt and pepper. Mix in cheese. Pour egg mixture over bacon/potato mixture.

Bake until set in the centre. Allow 35 minutes and leave to cool for 20 minutes. Cut into slices.

✳ Serve warm or at room temperature with a salad.

PARSNIP CHIP, BACON AND BLUE CHEESE SALAD

With autumn in the air it is time to start celebrating root vegetables. Combining the crunch of parsnip chips with the full-bodied flavour of blue cheese in a walnut/bacon-enhanced salad is quite delicious! **Serves 4**

125g blue cheese
2 tblsp coarsely chopped
 toasted walnuts
300g bacon rashers, rind
 removed, cut into 2cm pieces
2 medium parsnips, peeled
 and thinly sliced using a
 mandolin or vegetable peeler
 then soaked in cold water for
 15 minutes
vegetable or corn oil for
 deep-frying
1/4 cup extra virgin olive oil
1 tblsp sherry vinegar
1 tsp Dijon mustard
200g salad greens

METHOD

Combine the cheese and walnuts and mix well. Cover and refrigerate until needed.

Heat a non-stick frypan over medium heat, add bacon and cook for 5 minutes or until crisp. Drain on kitchen paper towels.

Drain parsnips and dry in a salad spinner or tea towel. Heat oil in a wok or deep-fryer to 160°C or when a piece of parsnip sizzles when dropped into the oil. Deep-fry 4–6 parsnip rounds at a time for 1 minute or until just golden, turning halfway during the cooking time.

Drain on absorbent paper and keep warm in oven. Repeat with remaining parsnip.

Whisk together olive oil, vinegar and mustard in a bowl and season to taste.

Combine salad leaves, bacon and parsnip chips. Add spoonfuls of the cheese mixture to salad, pour dressing over, toss gently to coat well and serve immediately.

PARMESAN-CRUSTED FISH WITH PARMESAN TOMATOES

Grated Parmesan cheese is the perfect addition to this versatile breadcrumb mixture. It provides the punchy piquancy and great all-over flavour! **Serves 4**

8 small fish fillets (we used
 John Dory fillets)
1 cup fresh breadcrumbs
1 cup grated Parmesan
1/2 cup chopped parsley
2 tblsp finely chopped thyme
sea salt and freshly ground
 black pepper
1/4 cup milk
2 eggs
1 cup flour
1/2 cup olive oil

METHOD

Place the fish fillets on a board.

Mix the breadcrumbs, Parmesan cheese, herbs and seasoning in a bowl. Lightly beat the milk and eggs in another bowl. Place flour in a flat dish.

Dip the fish in the flour, then the egg wash and finally in the breadcrumb mixture. Continue until all the fish is coated.

Rest in the fridge to for 30 minutes.

Heat oil in a large non-stick frypan over medium heat. Place fish in frypan in a single layer, taking care not to crowd too many pieces into the pan at one time. Cook for 1–2 minutes each side. Remove from the pan and keep warm until all the fish fillets are cooked.

✳ Serve the fish with Parmesan tomatoes. Simply cook tomato halves in a slow oven with a sprinkle of olive oil, sea salt and a little splash of balsamic vinegar for 2 hours. In the last 10–15 minutes, sprinkle liberally with grated Parmesan cheese.

✳ Serve fish with a cucumber salad – chopped cucumber, red onion and herb vinaigrette.

✳ Please note you cannot substitute the Parmesan cheese for any other grated cheese as the distinctive flavour and texture of this cheese works well with the breadcrumb coating.

✳ This is a versatile Parmesan breadcrumb mix – you can substitute chicken or your favourite seafood for the fish. Delicious with mussels.

heavenly mustard

Inspired by my trip to France and enjoying a collection of French mustards, I started to get busy with this versatile condiment. Forget mustard as just the optional extra for the white bread and ham sandwich – that is only the beginning …

'A tale without love is like beef without mustard: an insipid dish.' ANATOLE FRANCE, FRENCH HUMORIST

Tomato and mustard are happy bedfellows. For a fresh tomato tart, smear mustard over circles of puff pastry and then top with tomatoes, a hint of anchovy and a few olives and bake in a moderate oven. And a mustard dressing over sun-ripened tomato slices is heavenly: combine 1 tblsp Dijon mustard with 1 tblsp white or red wine vinegar and a pinch of salt in a bowl. Stir in 3 tblsp sunflower oil with a fork or whisk slowly (but constantly). Use the same ratio for extra tomatoes. Drizzle the dressing over the tomatoes and season with freshly ground black pepper and chopped fresh herbs. Serve with fresh crusty bread.

THE MUSTARD FILE

✳ If you are pressed for time – just combine 3 tblsp wholegrain mustard with 1/2 cup liquid honey or maple syrup and smear over chicken and place in a casserole or baking dish and simply roast in the oven. Yum!

✳ Another super chicken suggestion is to combine 1/2 cup honey with 1/4 cup Dijon mustard and 1 tsp curry powder. Smear over 1.5kg chicken pieces. Bake at 180°C for 1 hour.

✳ Improve the flavour of your own home-made cheeseburgers. Mix 1 tblsp Dijon mustard into 500g mince before forming patties. After cooking, spread additional Dijon mustard on the patties before topping with cheese. Grill to melt the cheese.

✳ Combine 750g hot steamed carrots with 1 tblsp honey, 1/2 tsp Dijon mustard, 11/2 tsp curry powder, 1 tblsp butter and 1 tsp brown sugar and serve.

✳ Steam new season's asparagus and serve with a bowl of honey-ginger mustard. To make honey-ginger mustard, combine 2 tblsp Colman's mustard powder with 1 tblsp cold water to form a smooth paste. Let it sit for 20 minutes. Place in a food processor with 3/4 cup Dijon mustard, 5 tblsp honey, 1 tsp grated fresh ginger and 1/4 cup ginger in syrup (very finely chopped ginger in syrup is found in supermarket bulk bins). Process until smooth. Store in sealed jar in fridge.

✳ Take a corner piece of beef topside (must be a corner piece) and smother with 100ml Dijon mustard, dot with butter and season with salt and pepper. Roast for 60 minutes at 200°C. Allow the meat to rest 15–20 minutes before serving. Delicious to slice thinly and make roast beef sandwiches for a crowd.

✳ To make a simple mustard vinaigrette to top warm steamed broccoli or new season's potatoes – just combine 2 heaped tblsp of wholegrain mustard with 1/4 cup white wine vinegar and 3/4 cup extra virgin olive oil. Add 1/4 cup chopped fresh herbs and season with salt and pepper.

✳ Mustard is an emulsifier. Add enough mustard to a salad dressing and it will help hold the oil and vinegar together. It can also minimise the possibility of curdling when used in a Hollandaise sauce.

✳ If someone describes you as 'the chief mustard maker' it is not a compliment. Historically, it means a vain and stupid person. Pope John XXII appointed a lazy and arrogant nephew to this position, and the negative association derives from that appointment.

MAPLE DIJON GLAZED CHICKEN
Don't let this unusual combination put you off – it's delicious and the aroma from the oven when it is cooking is just sensational! Serves 4

1/2 cup Dijon mustard
3 tsp white wine
1/4 tsp Worcestershire sauce
freshly ground black pepper
1 tsp diced onion
3 tsp pure maple syrup
4 chicken breast halves

METHOD
Preheat the grill. Combine all ingredients in a small bowl and blend well. Brush over the chicken and place on the grill, continuing to brush with glaze from time to time. Grill the chicken until cooked.

TARRAGON MUSTARD CHICKEN BREASTS
Serves 2-4

2 cups dry breadcrumbs
1/2 tsp salt
1/2 tsp paprika (optional)
freshly ground black pepper to taste
1 egg
4 tblsp Dijon mustard
2 shallots, peeled
2 tblsp dried tarragon
125g melted butter
**4 single chicken breasts, skinned,
 boned and slightly flattened**

SAUCE
2 tblsp Dijon mustard
2 shallots
1 tsp dried tarragon
1/4 cup chicken stock
1/2 cup dry white wine
2 tblsp butter
2 tsp finely chopped parsley

METHOD
In a small bowl mix together the breadcrumbs, salt, paprika (optional) and black pepper. Combine well. Set aside. In the food processor combine the egg, mustard, shallots and tarragon.

Add the melted butter in a thin steady stream and blend until the mixture is light and fluffy. Put in a bowl. Dip the chicken breasts into the mustard mixture, coating well. Roll in the breadcrumbs and fan-bake at 220°C for 15–20 minutes or until cooked. Test with a skewer to ensure the juices run clear.

To make the sauce
Place all the ingredients (except the butter and chopped parsley) in a food processor and blend until smooth.

Place in a pot and reduce by half. Whisk in the butter, 1 tblsp at a time. Keep warm. Serve over chicken and sprinkle with chopped parsley.

MEAT LOAF WITH ROASTED HAZEL-NUT AND FRESH TOMATO SAUCE

Try this simple, honest dinner and you will be delighted with the results! Any leftovers will be good cold the next day with chutney and pickles. Serves 4

2 slices toast bread
500g lean minced beef
1 medium egg
1/2 large onion, finely chopped
1 tblsp Worcestershire sauce
1–2 tblsp chopped fresh coriander or parsley
generous slurp of sweet Thai chilli sauce
1/2 capsicum, diced
2 carrots, grated
salt and freshly ground black pepper

FOR THE SAUCE:
2–3 large tomatoes
2–3 cloves garlic, peeled but left whole
1 red chilli, halved and deseeded (optional)
100g blanched hazelnuts
4 tblsp olive oil
1 tblsp sherry or chardonnay vinegar
2 tblsp chopped fresh coriander or parsley
salt and freshly ground black pepper

METHOD

For the meat loaf, place the bread into the food processor and whirl, then place in a large bowl with all the other ingredients, seasoning well with salt and pepper. Spoon the mixture into a lightly greased loaf tin and press down well.

Cover loosely with foil and bake at 150°C for 50–60 minutes. Remove from the oven and leave to cool for at least 20 minutes, then carefully drain away any liquid and turn out the meat loaf.

For the sauce, cut each tomato into 4 thick slices and place in a baking pan with the garlic, chilli and hazelnuts. Drizzle over half the oil and place in the oven with the meat loaf. Check after 30 minutes. When the tomatoes are soft they are ready to make the sauce. Tip tomatoes with garlic, chilli and hazelnuts into a blender or food processor and whizz briefly. Add remaining oil, vinegar and coriander. Whizz again until smooth and creamy. Season and pour into a bowl, then heat in the microwave for 30–60 seconds when ready to serve the slices of meat loaf.

✱ To serve – place a generous spoonful of mashed potatoes, flecked with chopped parsley, on a plate. Place the slices of warm meat loaf over the potatoes and spoon the sauce to one side of the meat loaf. Serve with steamed green vegetables and a carrot and parsnip mash.

✱ If you have pork mince as well as beef, you can use it in this recipe. With all the other ingredients the same, the meat component can go up to 700g without any problems – just adjust the cooking time.

Witlof is a relatively recent arrival on the vegetable scene and was only discovered in the 1800s. It gives salads the most unique, delicious flavour that will delight you, but it does need just a little special handling. Keep the dark wrapper it is stored in around the vegetable until you use it – otherwise it will discolour and become bitter. Here are two variations on a theme for a great winter's lunch. Serve a salad and a bowl of soup and bread, then a slice of warm cake for dessert, and lunch is complete!

CAMEMBERT, PEAR, WITLOF AND WALNUT SALAD

Delicious with cooked pork or ham. This is a great combination of creamy, full-flavoured cheese, the bitter contrast of the witlof and the sweetness of the grapes and pears. Always ensure the Camembert is at room temperature before you slice it.

1 230g Camembert cheese, cut into thin slices
3 pears, segmented
1 lemon (to drizzle over pears)
3 witlof, leaves separated
1 bunch mizuna or soft salad greens, trimmed
1 cup toasted walnuts
1 cup seedless grapes
1 tblsp chardonnay vinegar
1 tsp wholegrain mustard
3 tblsp extra virgin olive oil
salt and freshly ground black pepper

METHOD
Remove the Camembert from the fridge and allow to reach room temperature before using, ideally on a warm sunny kitchen bench. Core and thinly slice the pears. Squeeze the juice from the lemon over the pears.

Remove the end of the witlof and the core, if necessary. Gently peel off the leaves.

Combine the first 7 ingredients together in a bowl, then blend together the vinegar with the mustard and drizzle in the oil. Season and toss through the salad.

Place dressed salad on a white plate and serve immediately.

✳ Remember that light makes the witlof go green and bitter – so keep it out of light by covering with the dark blue/purple paper it is transported in.

GRUYÈRE WITLOF SALAD

When you travel to France and visit a busy wine bar or café at lunch time, there are always scores of people eating a mixed green salad with cubes of Swiss cheese and ham. The salad greens glisten with dressing and the basket of bread mops up all the juices. A hint of mustard in the salad dressing brings perfection to this simple lunch option. Our Gruyère cheese is the perfect cheese to use in this salad. Enjoy the salad as it is, or add cubes of ham. It's also delicious with pork or chicken.

3 oranges, segmented
1 avocado, peeled, stoned and sliced
1 witlof, leaves separated
1 bunch mizuna, trimmed, or assorted salad greens
100g Gruyère cheese cut into thin slices or cubed
1 tblsp chardonnay vinegar
1 tsp wholegrain mustard
3 tblsp extra virgin olive oil
salt and freshly ground black pepper

METHOD
Combine the first 5 ingredients together in a bowl and then blend together the vinegar with the mustard and drizzle in the oil. Season and toss through the salad.

When it comes to winter vegetables my heart always goes out to turnips. Much maligned, misunderstood, taken for granted and unceremoniously labelled 'cattle fodder' – they are never showcased. Peppy waiters with fancy aprons do not wax lyrical about a turnip purée 'that you simply must try' and I've never heard anyone admit turnips were their favourite vegetable. When it comes to competition with potatoes, kumara and pumpkin, they just don't have a chance. More is the pity, and it's time to readdress the issue. Turnips are simply delicious when handled correctly, and the baby turnip is a very sexy vegetable indeed.

✱ Try baby turnips with other baby vegetables: steam or cook lightly in boiling water, then finish them off in the oven or in a large frypan with a knob of butter until coloured.

✱ Or simply cook completely in a heavy pan with unsalted butter and sprigs of fresh thyme. When lightly coloured add chicken stock and cook over heat until the stock evaporates. Serve with a roasted leg of lamb or duck.

✱ The leafy tops of turnips, once well washed and lightly cooked, are also edible.

✱ Turnips play an important role with many well-known dishes. They can feature in an Irish stew, the traditional New England boiled beef dinner, the French classic veal stew, Blanquette de Veau, and can make an appearance in a hearty seafood chowder or a Moroccan-style chicken dish.

✱ When buying turnips, go for firm and not soft, small rather than large and woody. Store them lightly wrapped in plastic in the vegetable bin in the fridge; they will keep for weeks. Turnips need to be peeled before cooking, even the small ones, in case there is any bitterness in the skin. Turnips are best simmered in liquid until tender but not waterlogged, then roasted until soft. With baby turnips, try steaming and tossing them in melted butter with a little honey. Season with salt and pepper and serve.

✱ Make creamy turnip soup. Melt 3 tblsp butter in a heavy large stockpot over a medium heat, add 2 sliced leeks and 1 sliced onion and sauté for about 12 minutes until onion is translucent. Add 5 sliced, peeled turnips and 1 sliced, peeled potato and sauté for 2 minutes, then add 5 cups chicken stock and bring to boil. Reduce heat to low and simmer for about 30 minutes until vegetables are very tender. Whizz soup, return to pot and add 2 cups milk and a small splash of cream (optional). Bring back to a simmer and season with nutmeg and salt and pepper. Serve. Decorate with chopped chives, if desired.

✱ If you enjoy all vegetables, you will love combining cooked turnips with Brussels sprouts and golden beets. Add shallots, hazelnuts and thyme for a stunning combination. Cook Brussels sprouts in a steamer until just cooked, the same with the baby turnips or pieces of a large turnip, and wrap beets in foil and bake until tender in oven. Allow nearly 1½–2 hours for the beets. Melt butter in large frypan, add minced shallots and soften, then stir in chopped hazelnuts, fresh thyme and all the vegetables. Season with salt and freshly ground black pepper and serve.

✱ Make rustic mashed turnips with nutmeg. Toss turnips in butter and sprinkle with salt and pepper. Cover dish with foil. Bake at 170°C for about 1 hour until tender. Remove from oven and mash coarsely. Stir in nutmeg and season to taste with salt and pepper.

ROAST VEGETABLE PASTA

Even if you are not a vegetarian, it's a good idea to make a couple of meals a week meatless. This roast vegetable pasta is simply delicious and positively light. Instead of a heavy sauce, you spoon cottage cheese into the pasta – it's delicious. Yum. **Serves 4**

800g vegetables (including pumpkin,
 parsnip and kumara)
olive oil
sea salt and freshly ground black pepper
fresh rosemary
250g cooked pasta
250g Garlic Cottage Cheese and Chives
1/2 cup toasted cashews or pinenuts
3 spring onions, chopped
2 tblsp lemon olive oil
salt and freshly ground black pepper

METHOD

Prepare vegetables for roasting. Cut into 2cm chunks to ensure speedy cooking. Place vegetables on an oven tray and drizzle with olive oil. Sprinkle sea salt, pepper and fresh rosemary over the tray and roast at 200ºC for 20 minutes.

Cook the pasta according to the instructions on the packet. Combine cooked pasta with cottage cheese and nuts. Fold in roasted vegetables, spring onions and a drizzle of lemon oil.

Season to taste and serve with shaved Parmesan.

CHICKEN WITH CRANBERRY AND MUSTARD SAUCE

With the full and captivating flavours of cranberry, a hint of orange and the piquancy of Dijon mustard all combined in a creamy sauce, this is perfect to serve over noodles, rice or mashed potatoes. **Serves 4**

4 boneless chicken breast halves with skin
2 tblsp chopped fresh lemon thyme
 or 3 tsp dried thyme
2 tblsp olive oil
1/4 cup whole berry cranberry sauce
1/2 cup chicken stock
1/2 cup orange juice
2–3 tblsp Dijon mustard
4 tblsp crème fraîche
salt and freshly ground black pepper

METHOD

Sprinkle chicken with thyme, salt and pepper. Heat oil in heavy large frypan over medium high heat. Add chicken and cook for about 3 minutes per side until brown. Transfer chicken to plate. Add all remaining ingredients to pan and bring to the boil, scraping up any browned bits and whisking to blend well. Reduce heat to medium and simmer for about 7 minutes until sauce thickens enough to coat a spoon. Return chicken to pan and simmer for about 6 minutes until just cooked through, turning occasionally. Season to taste with salt and pepper. Transfer chicken and sauce to plates and serve. Return chicken to pan and simmer for about 6 minutes until cooked through. Season with salt and pepper.

ROOT VEGETABLE GRATIN

This is the perfect dish for a special dinner party – a real showcase for Gruyère cheese! The combination of the natural nutty flavour of the cheese and these much-maligned root vegetables is just great! Good news for home cooks – you can prepare ahead. **Serves 4**

2 swedes
1 medium turnip
4 medium parsnips
2 tblsp flour
11/4 cups grated Gruyère cheese
salt and freshly ground black pepper
1 cup cream
1 cup milk

METHOD

Peel and prepare the vegetables.

Slice the vegetables thinly – the food processor is ideal for this. Cook until just tender either by steaming or microwaving. Preheat the oven to 180°C. Butter a gratin dish.

Arrange half of the vegetables over the bottom of the dish, and sprinkle with 1 tblsp flour, 1/2 cup Gruyère cheese and salt and pepper to taste. Repeat next layer. Pour cream and milk over vegetables.

Sprinkle remaining cheese (1/4 cup) over the vegetables and bake for 30 minutes, covered, in the middle of the oven. Uncover and bake for about 40 minutes more until bubbling and golden.

ROAST FENNEL

Make sure you turn the fennel during cooking or it will brown only on one side. This is delicious with roasted lamb and chicken, and also great with chargrilled fish and seafood generally.

3–4 large fennel bulbs
5–6 tblsp olive oil
salt and freshly ground
 black pepper

METHOD
Trim the top of the fennel and remove any tough outer layers. Cut the fennel into quarters and rinse under cold running water, then pat dry thoroughly. Place in a small roasting dish and pour over oil. Season with salt and pepper and turn the fennel pieces to coat them well in the oil. Roast in a 230°C oven for about 25 minutes or until tender, basting and turning once. Serve warm with pan juices.

FENNEL SALAD

Search out a good produce supplier for fennel bulbs and make this winter salad to accompany fish. Fennel is also very good in a seafood risotto, but try this simple recipe first. It comes from inspirational Australian chef, Bill Marchetti, in Melbourne.

1 fennel bulb, thinly sliced
salt
2 tblsp tarragon leaves
10 Ligurian olives
50ml champagne vinegar
100ml premium extra virgin
 olive oil
freshly ground black pepper

METHOD
Sprinkle the fennel with ample salt, then leave it for about 30 minutes until the fennel softens. Rinse off the excess salt. Add the rest of the ingredients and toss well.

Serve with grilled white meat or fish.

CAULIFLOWER CHEESE AND PASTA

The cheese in this recipe gives it the bold and hearty flavour this classic dish needs. With the pasta combined with an all-time favourite – cauliflower and cheese – the whole family will be delighted. Delicious with a drizzle of sweet Thai chilli sauce.

8 cups water
6 cups cauliflower florets
3/4 tsp salt
250g uncooked small
 seashell pasta
drizzle of olive oil
generous knob of butter
1/4 cup flour
3 cups milk
3 cloves garlic, minced
2 tsp chopped fresh or
 3/4 tsp dried thyme
1/4 tsp salt
1 cup grated tasty Cheddar
 cheese
1/2 cup grated Parmesan
3/4 cup spring onions, chopped
2 tsp Dijon mustard
1/4 tsp black pepper
2 slices white bread for
 breadcrumbs
2 tsp butter, melted
4 rashers bacon strips

METHOD
Preheat the oven to 200°C. Bring the water to a boil, add salt and cook cauliflower for 2–3 minutes until just tender.

Remove the cauliflower from the water and reheat the 'cauli water'.

Cook the pasta in this water according to packet instructions, drain and set aside with a drizzle of oil. Heat the butter, add the flour and cook out the flour until it turns a golden colour. Add milk and stir with a whisk. Add garlic and thyme and cook for about 8 minutes over a medium heat until thick. Stir constantly.

Remove from the heat and add 1/4 tsp salt and the cheeses, spring onions, mustard and pepper. Combine cauliflower, pasta and cheese sauce in a large bowl.

Spoon mixture into a greased casserole. Top with fresh bread-crumbs, butter and bacon strips.

Bake at 200°C for 20 minutes.

✱ Sliced fresh fennel is delicious added to a potato soup or potato salad, or even a pot of mussels.

✱ Fennel and orange make a great addition to chargrilled fish. Sauté slices of fresh fennel (allow 8 minutes in a frypan with a light coating of olive oil) and then cover for another 8-10 minutes so they are softened and lightly coloured. Add the juice of one orange, diced orange segments and then season. Serve over fish.

✱ Add finely diced fresh raw fennel, some fennel seeds, diced shallot and olive oil to a bowl of chopped tomatoes. Season well and serve on top of sourdough toast. Superb!

WINTER DESSERTS

STICKY DATE PUDDING

This is the best sticky date pudding ever, and as it is a classic it needs to be highlighted and celebrated in all its glory. Serve with lashings of caramel sauce, or custard and cream!

1¹/2 cups dates, chopped
1 tsp baking soda
1¹/4 cups boiling water
75g butter
1 cup brown sugar (firmly packed)
1 tsp vanilla essence
grated rind and juice of 1 orange
2 large eggs
1 cup flour
1¹/4 tsp baking powder
250ml custard
cream

METHOD

Place the dates in a bowl and sprinkle with soda, then pour over the boiling water. Stir until soda is dissolved and allow to stand for 15 minutes.

Cream butter and sugar. Add vanilla, orange rind and eggs one at a time, beating well after each addition.

Sift flour and baking powder. Fold into the butter mixture. Add the date mixture and the orange juice and stir to combine (this mixture will be very sloppy).

Pour the mixture into a greased and lined 20cm spring-form cake tin. Bake at 175°C for 40–50 minutes or until a skewer is inserted and comes out cleanly. Remove pudding from oven and let stand for 10 minutes before removing from pan onto a serving platter.

Serve immediately with custard and cream or heated caramel sauce.

✱ To make a simple caramel sauce, heat 50g butter in a pan with 50g (approximately 3–4 tblsp) brown sugar. Melt, stir together and slowly add 1 cup cream. Heat through gently.

EVERGREEN LODGE ALMOND PANFORTE

Another recipe from John at Evergreen Lodge in Queenstown.

50g butter
1 can (397g) sweetened condensed milk
1 tsp almond essence
1 cup desiccated coconut
1/2 cup whole chocolate melts
1 cup whole blanched almonds
1/2 cup chopped dried apricots
1/2 cup sultanas
1/2 cup whole hazelnuts
1/2 cup chopped crystallised ginger
2 cups ground almonds
1/2 cup chopped dates
1/2 cup chopped dried figs

METHOD

Melt together the first 3 ingredients. In a large bowl place all the other ingredients, then pour over the melted mixture and combine. Press into a large greased and lined baking tray and bake at 180°C for 40 minutes. Cool, and store in the fridge.

Slice thinly as needed – delicious with coffee at the end of a meal!

APRICOT, CRANBERRY AND WALNUT PIE

This is a quick and easy dessert – a perfect full-fruit pie to help celebrate a mid-winter Christmas. The craisins (sweetened dried cranberries) contrast perfectly with the full apricot flavour, and the walnuts provide texture. When we made it on television we were inundated with praise for this wondrous combination. **Serves 8**

1 23cm sweet short pastry pie crust (unbaked)
1 cup brown sugar
2 large eggs
1 tsp vanilla extract
1/4 cup cream
3 tblsp butter, melted
1 tsp ground cinnamon
1¹/2 cups coarsely chopped walnuts
1¹/2 cups dried apricots (about 225g),
 cut into 1.25cm pieces
1 cup craisins
additional craisins, dried apricots
 and walnuts for garnish

METHOD

Position rack in centre of oven and preheat oven to 190°C. Whisk brown sugar, eggs and vanilla extract in large bowl to blend. Whisk in cream, melted butter and cinnamon, then stir in chopped walnuts, apricot pieces and craisins.

Transfer filling to prepared crust. Bake for about 1 hour until filling is set and crust is golden, tenting pie with foil if crust browns too quickly. Transfer pie to rack; cool pie completely. Serve with ice-cream or whipped cream.

Apricot, cranberry and walnut pie

If your destination is South Australia, do leave time to explore the delightful Clare Valley. Many visitors enjoy the European charm and great wineries in the Barossa Valley but do not venture that little bit further to the Clare Valley, which is a pity because the undulating, less-travelled Clare Valley is charming.

David and Michael

The home of great flinty rieslings and Thorn Park Country House, near the little township of Sevenhill, is reason enough to visit the area. Thorn Park is set on grounds with tranquil vistas of rolling farmland studded with towering gums and grazing cattle, and an 1850s homestead that has been extensively restored in recent years to its original grandeur. The garden has hawthorn and elm trees, and exquisite roses.

My weekend visit to Thorn Park, with hosts David Hay and Michael Speers, was a personal delight and a source of great culinary inspiration. Michael is the perfect host, charming, easily guiding guests from one gastronomic delight to another with warmth and humour. Equally personable, David is a stellar chef with a generosity of spirit and great sense of fun. You arrive to a pot of tea and jars of home-made cookies, with the aroma of bread and simmering sauces and stocks. Then, after a rest or wine tour, comes a sumptuous dinner with your fellow guests. Our first night menu consisted of prawns with carrot and coconut salad, twice-cooked duck with wild rice and spring onion pancakes followed by poached quinces with anise and coconut ice-cream.

The next morning we were served the house muesli and a luscious compote of dried fruits with yoghurt and then a perfectly cooked traditional breakfast – even kedgeree on Sunday mornings. The home-made bread toasted on the Aga stove was served with lashings of home-made preserves.

Thorn Park in winter is special. Dry, bright blue days, with autumn colour still evident and crackling fires in the living room. Country feel with an easy sophistication – a charming, aesthetic experience. A longer stay next time is needed. This is a real treasure, seek it out!

PARSNIP AND CORIANDER CUSTARD

David makes these savoury custards on a regular basis. They are so easy and always work – for a small group to a large banquet – and best of all, they are perfectly portion controlled! Makes about 10 small custards.

500g peeled parsnips
75g melted butter
1 tsp ground cumin
2 tblsp chopped coriander
150ml cream
4 eggs
salt and freshly ground black pepper to taste

METHOD

Peel and slice the parsnips and steam until just cooked. In the melted butter sauté parsnips with ground cumin and chopped coriander.

Cool, then purée with cream and eggs, and check for seasonings.

Place in buttered ramekins and cook in a water bath for 20–30 minutes at 180°C or until firm.

These custards can be made ahead of time and reheated in a water bath or in covered foil containers.

WILD RICE AND SPRING ONION PANCAKES

These were delicious with the roast duck, but would be equally delicious with pork, chicken or even chargrilled seafood. Makes about 24

1¹/2 cups flour
1 tsp baking powder
1 tsp sea salt
1/2 tsp ground Szechwan pepper
1¹/2 cups milk
3 egg yolks
3 tblsp melted butter
70g wild rice, cooked and well drained
1 cup chopped spring onions,
  white and green parts
3 egg whites

METHOD

Mix all the dry ingredients together, add the milk and the egg yolks and blend well.

Mix in the melted butter, then the rice and spring onions. Check seasoning.

Just before serving, beat the egg whites to soft peaks and fold into batter.

Heat a non-stick pan, grease it lightly and pour in a tablespoon of batter. Cook on a medium heat until a light golden colour. Turn over and cook the other side until coloured – this will not take long. Keep warm until needed.

TOASTED MUESLI

This recipe does make a generous batch, so adjust it accordingly, and if you prefer to reduce the amount of almonds, then do so. Make sure none of the nuts are salty.

250mls honey
100mls vegetable oil (peanut or similar)
500g roughly chopped whole unblanched almonds
125g chopped pecans
75g roughly chopped cashews
75g roughly chopped blanched pistachios
75g sunflower seeds
250g rolled oats
350g toasted wheat or bran flakes
  (or packet of toasted muesli)
75g coarse desiccated coconut
200g currants
50g wheatgerm
100g chopped apricots
yoghurt to serve
fresh fruit of your choice or stewed
  or poached fruits

METHOD

Warm the honey and oil together until completely melted. Mix this with the nut and grain mix and spread evenly over several high-sided baking dishes. Slowly roast in a preheated oven at 150°C until golden and crisp – this should take about 30–40 minutes, but check the oven every 10–15 minutes to ensure that it is not burning. Mix well when you are checking it. Remove from oven and mix through the flakes, coconut and currants whilst warm, then leave to cool.

Store in airtight containers.

To serve the most amazing breakfast, place several generous dollops of yoghurt into a bowl, top with this scrumptious muesli and garnish with fresh fruit.

favourite dishes

We all have our signature dishes, the food we can prepare on autopilot. The recipes are familiar and they are much loved by those near to us. These dishes reassure and soothe ... they are simple, easy and approachable.

✱ A spoonful of home-made chutney or relish delights a plain cheese sandwich, livens up a roast and makes many favourite dishes spring with vibrant flavour. A passion for chutney is not a bad thing.

HAMISH'S RHUBARB AND GINGER CHUTNEY

Chef Hamish Brown loves to make pickles and preserves in his busy kitchen at the George Hotel in Christchurch. One of his favourites is this simple combination of rhubarb and ginger. Try it with grilled chicken or roast turkey.

100g onion
4 cloves garlic
50g fresh ginger
400g rhubarb
cooking oil
25g (1–2 tblsp) tomato paste
30ml Worcestershire sauce
40g (about 2 tblsp) brown sugar
100ml red wine vinegar
salt and freshly ground black pepper

METHOD
Cut the onion into 1/2cm dice, crush the garlic and grate the ginger. Cut the rhubarb into 1cm strips and wash well. Sauté the onion, ginger and garlic in a little cooking oil on a low heat to maximise the intensity of the natural sweetness of the onion.

Add the rhubarb and sauté for 2–3 minutes. Add the remaining ingredients and stir until all the sugar has dissolved and the rhubarb is tender. Place in a small bowl and cover with plastic wrap and allow to cool.

At this point, season with salt and pepper according to your taste. Keep the chutney in the fridge and make small amounts like this often, rather than a larger amount, less often.

Chutney should be served at room temperature.

MUSHROOM PARMESAN RISOTTO

Serve this simple risotto with a mixed green salad and red wine vinaigrette. It provides colour, crunch and contrast of flavour – the acidity of the salad versus the creamy, earthy flavours of the wild mushroom risotto are superb. The full flavour of the Parmesan adds piquancy to this dish! Serves 2–3

3 cups vegetable stock
1 cup dry white wine
2 tblsp butter
250g sliced fresh mixed wild mushrooms
 (such as shiitake and oyster)
2 tblsp chopped fresh thyme or 2 tsp dried
1 cup arborio rice
1/4–1/2 cup Parmesan
salt and freshly ground black pepper

METHOD
Bring stock and wine to a simmer in a heavy saucepan. Cover pan and keep warm. Melt butter in a frypan over medium heat. Add mushrooms and 1 tblsp thyme and sauté for about 3 minutes until mushrooms soften. Mix in rice. Add a cup of hot stock and stir until stock has been absorbed, then add all remaining stock except for 1/4 cup. Reduce heat to medium. Simmer uncovered for about 15–18 minutes, stirring occasionally, until rice is almost tender. Add remaining stock and simmer, stirring occasionally, for about 5 minutes. Stir in cheese and 1 tblsp thyme.

Season with salt and pepper.

✱ Place risotto in a large, white, bistro-style serving bowl and top with slices of warm bacon-wrapped lamb fillets topped with dressed salad greens. To make this simple delicious treatment of lamb tenderloin fillets, remove any silverskin on the meat and smear meat with your favourite wholegrain mustard. Wrap fillets in bacon strips and cook on a hot grill for 4–5 minutes only, then leave to rest for 2–4 minutes before slicing. Equally delicious sliced and placed over a platter of chargrilled vegetables with feta cheese and mint vinaigrette.

Israeli couscous is a new favourite in the kitchen, but confusion reigns amongst the grains and starches. Just when you could identify your couscous (granular semolina) from your bulgur wheat (steamed, dried and crushed wheat kernels), your polenta (cornmeal) from your quinoa (South American grain) and your amaranth (high-protein seeds) from your kamut (high-protein wheat), along came Israeli couscous.

Israeli couscous is now extremely fashionable with chefs, appearing on menus as a base for a braise or stew, gracing a salad or combined very effectively with chargrilled vegetables and becoming a main course. Invented in the 1950s by the Tel Aviv-based firm Osem, Israeli couscous is extruded (like ordinary pasta) and toasted to dry (like Jewish farfel). When cooked, the result is a chewy, buttery carbohydrate that is shaped more like pearls of tapioca than actual couscous, and over the years it has become a staple in Israel. To make matters more confusing, traditional African couscous is often mistakenly referred to as a grain. In fact, it is a method of treating durum semolina (the same wheat used to make pasta) that produces small granules, which are then steamed several times and fluffed.

Israeli couscous has a nuttier flavour and is clearly a more substantial version than its more familiar African (or otherwise known as Moroccan) counterpart, the tiny grain-like pasta found in a box in the supermarket.

Israeli couscous is neutral-tasting and combines well with sweet or savoury flavours. The beads of pasta absorb the flavours of whatever liquids they are paired with, from chicken or vegetable stock to fruit juices. It is most often found as a side dish for meat and poultry, but, in the Middle Eastern tradition of stuffed vegetables, also makes a perfect filling for courgettes, pumpkin or roasted capsicums. You may also want to experiment with using prepared Israeli couscous as a stuffing for chicken, as the grains soak up flavour without becoming soggy. The pasta is delicious when served at room temperature, making it an ideal ingredient in salads or pilafs for buffets or lunches. You can substitute prepared Israeli couscous for bulgur wheat in virtually any pilaf or tabbouleh recipe.

Israeli couscous does require different handling. While boxed instant couscous typically is prepared by adding boiling water and leaving it to absorb the liquid for a few minutes, Israeli couscous must be boiled like pasta. The process is quick, however; simply bring a large pot of water to a boil, add desired amount of couscous, and boil until the pasta is soft yet firm to the bite.

Prior to boiling, many restaurant chefs 'toast' the couscous with a few tablespooons of butter or olive oil and seasonings to bring out its nutty flavour – similar to making a risotto. The couscous is then boiled in stock or water until soft. This preparation produces a dish akin to orzo – the couscous pearls remain separate, but are bound together by a thin sauce.

SIMPLE ISRAELI COUSCOUS

2 tblsp extra virgin olive oil
1/2 cup minced onion
2–3 cloves garlic, minced
1 cup Israeli couscous
1/2 cup chardonnay
2 cups chicken stock
1/2 cup grated Parmesan cheese
1/2 cup chopped apricots
1/4 cup currants
freshly chopped parsley
coarse sea salt and freshly
 ground black pepper to taste

METHOD

In a small saucepan, sweat the onion and garlic in the olive oil until the onion is softened and translucent. Add the couscous, stir to coat, and brown lightly, stirring to prevent burning or sticking. Add wine and stir briefly. Add the stock, cover the pot tightly and reduce the heat to low until the couscous absorbs the stock and cooks through, about 20–30 minutes.

Add the cheese, dried fruits and chopped herbs and stir to combine. Season with salt and pepper and serve immediately. You can substitute any liquids or seasonings you like; the basic ratio is 1 cup couscous to 2 cups liquid.

* Make an Israeli couscous and corn salad. Combine cooked couscous, with fresh corn kernels, finely diced red onion, fresh coriander and mint, red capsicum and a lime-honey dressing. For the dressing, combine 1/3 cup lime juice with 1/4 cup extra virgin olive oil, 2 tblsp rice wine vinegar, 1 tblsp honey, 1/2-1 tsp finely grated lime zest and freshly ground black pepper and salt.

* Another delicious lunch suggestion is to cook Israeli couscous in a little olive oil, adding the water and lemon zest for flavour. When cooked add sautéed almonds, onion, snow peas and prawns. Add chopped spring onions, a good splash of sherry vinegar and a little olive oil, season and decorate with cherry tomatoes. Serve in lettuce cups.

* Another delicious combination is to combine cooked Israeli couscous with roasted pumpkin, a hint of cinnamon and scatter with sultanas, pinenuts, chopped parsley and thin slices of preserved lemon. Delicious with chargrilled fish and seafood generally.

AUGUST ... and delicious crusts

Adding a crust to a favourite piece of fish or even a simple chicken breast transforms the whole meal into something very smart indeed.

The essence of a delicious crust is all about texture. Too often we neglect crunchiness and mouth feel with food, concentrating mainly on balance, layering and contrast with flavours. Adding this extra dimension will improve the whole enjoyment of your food and is very straightforward. In most crust situations, there is a smear of French mustard (for flavour and to help the crust stick to the food) and then the topping is pressed on and the roasting or baking continues as per normal. Remember, the whole process should be simple – don't overdo the herbs or spices, just keep it manageable and light.

BAKED FISH WITH ORANGE AND HERB CRUST

This dinner dish hardly requires any preparation – the food processor does most of the work.
Serves 4

4 boneless, skinless fish fillets about 140g each
2 tblsp olive oil, plus extra for greasing
8 slices white bread, no crusts
small handful fresh parsley
salt and freshly ground black pepper
finely grated zest of 1 orange
1 small red chilli, seeded and finely chopped
TO SERVE:
buttered steamed new potatoes or
 oven-roasted potatoes
steamed green beans
orange or lemon wedges

METHOD
Preheat the oven to 220°C. Put the fish fillets on a lightly oiled baking sheet. Tear the bread into the food processor, then sprinkle in the parsley and salt and pepper and process until finely chopped. Tip the crumbs into a bowl and stir in the oil, orange zest and chilli.

Press the mixture on top of the fish fillets. Bake for around 12 minutes or until the fish is cooked and the topping is golden. Serve with potatoes, beans and orange or lemon wedges.

* Jazz up that chicken breast by blending 1/2 cup pesto, 1/4 cup chopped walnuts, 2 tblsp lemon juice and 1 tsp grated lemon peel in the food processor until just combined. Place four chicken breasts in a baking dish. Coat chicken with pesto mixture and drizzle with oil. Bake chicken for about 30 minutes until cooked through. Transfer chicken to a platter and tent with foil. Strain pan juices into small bowl, pressing solids in strainer to extract as much liquid as possible. Whisk in another 2 tblsp lemon juice and season sauce to taste with salt and pepper. Spoon sauce over chicken. Garnish with lemon wedges and serve.

* The texture can also come in the form of a coating. Take 4 of your favourite pork steaks and give them star treatment. In pie dish mix 11/2 cups fresh breadcrumbs with 1 cup Parmesan cheese, 1 tblsp dried sage and 1 tsp grated lemon peel. Whisk 2 large eggs in medium bowl to blend. Place flour on plate and season generously with salt and pepper. Coat pork steaks on both sides with flour; shake off excess. Dip chops into eggs, then coat on both sides with breadcrumb mixture. Melt 2 tblsp butter with 2 tblsp olive oil in heavy large ovenproof skillet over medium high heat. Add pork steaks to pan and cook as per usual.

* Make a garlic herb crust for your next beef roast. With the food processor running, drop 4 garlic cloves into bowl and blend until finely chopped. Add 8 fresh sage leaves, 4 tsp thyme, 4 tsp olive oil and salt and pepper and process until paste forms. Pat meat dry with paper towels and rub meat all over with herb paste. Cover and chill for at least 3 hours. Bring back to room temperature and then roast as per usual. Sensational flavours!

* Another delicious beef crust is to combine 2 tsp crushed whole allspice berries, 3 tblsp lightly crushed dried pink peppercorns, 3 tblsp lightly crushed green peppercorns, 3 tblsp softened butter, 2 tblsp flour, 1 tblsp brown sugar, 1 tblsp Dijon mustard and 1 tsp salt. Smear all over the beef and roast as per usual. Another even simpler variation on this theme is to smear your 500g beef fillet with 2 tblsp seeded French mustard and then sprinkle the top with 1 tsp crushed dried pink peppercorns. Roast as per usual and then serve with a port, wine and redcurrant jelly sauce. Place 1/3 cup port, 1 cup red wine and 1 tblsp redcurrant jelly in a pot and simmer for at least 4-5 minutes until reduced by half.

* Anchovies crushed with olive oil can also be smeared all over your lamb roast before roasting and then topped with an olive crust towards the end of the cooking time. For an olive crust try combining in the food processor 3/4 cup de-stoned black Kalamata olives, 3 tblsp fresh breadcrumbs and 1 egg and press onto the lamb for the last 25-30 minutes of cooking.

* For your next rack of lamb for a special dinner, try this spinach and pinenut crust. Place 1 bunch of wilted and well-drained spinach into the food processor. Pulse spinach with 1/3 cup toasted pinenuts, 1/2 cup parsley, a couple of slices of ham (torn into pieces) and 30g butter until finely chopped. Transfer to a large bowl. Stir in 1 cup fresh breadcrumbs, 1 large egg, 1 tsp finely grated fresh lemon zest, 1/2 tsp salt and 1/4 tsp freshly ground black pepper. Smear trimmed and seared racks with French mustard and then place crust all over the lamb. Finish final cooking in the oven.

* Lamb and hazelnuts go well together. Combine 2 cups fresh breadcrumbs, 1/2 cup chopped parsley, 1/4 cup toasted hazelnuts and 1 large shallot in processor. Process until nuts are finely ground. Gradually add 2 tblsp oil and process until crumbs begin to stick together. Transfer to a bowl and season with salt and pepper. Add 1 tblsp oil and toss gently to coat. Smear your lamb with French mustard and then top with the crust. Roast or bake as per usual.

* Vegetables enjoy a crust and/or topping. Baked tomatoes enjoy a little flavour crust. Simply sauté several cloves of minced garlic in a little olive oil until soft but not coloured, then stir in 1/2 cup finely chopped parsley. Sprinkle on top of tomatoes and scatter a few toasted pinenuts on top. Tomatoes, like eggplant and potatoes, all enjoy being stuffed and enhanced with toppings or crusts. With tomatoes, the centres can be removed raw and added to cooked grains and herbs and refilled. Potatoes and eggplant can be cooked first, the filling removed and combined with cheese and herbs and a little onion and then topped with a herb-inspired breadcrumb mixture.

* Even desserts are enhanced with toppings and crusts. Stuffed peaches or nectarines are a popular Italian dessert. Mix 150g crumbed amaretti biscuits with 1 egg, 2 tblsp roughly chopped almonds and 2 tblsp brown sugar and pile into cavities of 6 peaches that have been halved and de-stoned. Arrange peaches in a baking dish, cavity side up, add 1 cup orange juice to the pan to keep the fruit moist while cooking and bake for 30 minutes at 180°C.

more favourites ...

PASTICCIO

This is perfect comfort food. Make ahead and serve warm, not hot, with a generous mixed green salad. Tastes better made one day ahead. **Serves 6–8**

MEAT SAUCE
1/2 cup chopped onions
oil
500g beef mince
1 jar pasta sauce
1/2 cup soft breadcrumbs
salt and freshly ground
 black pepper

PASTA
250g macaroni
drizzle of oil
chopped parsley
2 unbeaten egg whites
1/2 cup grated cheese

CHEESE SAUCE
2 tblsp butter
1/2 cup flour
13/4 cups milk
1/2 tsp nutmeg
salt and freshly ground
 black pepper
2 unbeaten egg yolks
1/3 cup grated cheese
extra grated cheese for the top

METHOD
Sauté the onions in oil, add mince and pasta sauce and cook slowly for 30–40 minutes. It should be a thick, not runny, sauce. Add breadcrumbs, season and reserve.

Boil macaroni, strain and drizzle with oil, and when cooled add the parsley, egg whites and 1/2 cup grated cheese. Reserve.

To make the cheese sauce, heat the butter and add the flour, blending well. Cook for a minute. Add milk and seasoning. When thick, add unbeaten egg yolks and 1/3 cup grated cheese.

Butter a casserole dish, put in the pasta, spread the meat sauce on top and cover with the thick cheese sauce. Top sauce with grated cheese and bake for 30–40 minutes at 180°C.

CLASSIC STEAMED PUDDING WITH CUSTARD

This is the classic winter steamed pudding, the dessert we all had as children and the perfect vehicle for lashings of custard!

1/3 cup golden syrup
200g softened butter
1/2 cup sugar
1/2 cup brown sugar
4 large eggs
1 tsp vanilla
1–2 tsp finely grated lemon rind
11/2–12/3 cups flour
11/4 tsp baking powder
4 tblsp milk
custard to serve

METHOD
Lightly grease and flour a 1.5 litre capacity pudding basin. Pour the golden syrup into the bottom of the basin. Cream the butter and sugars until light and fluffy. Beat in eggs one at a time, beating well after each addition. Add the vanilla and lemon rind and beat well. Sift the flour and baking powder and gently mix into the creamed mixture. Add the milk.

Pile the batter into the pudding basin, making sure the surface is level. Cover with a lid and steam for 2 hours in a large pot half-filled with simmering water and sealed with a tight-fitting lid.

Serve hot with custard.

✳ Heating the custard in the microwave is an easy option – for a jugful of 600ml custard just heat on high for 30–60 seconds, covered, and stir, then continue heating until warm.
✳ If you have buttermilk on hand, you can add a slurp to this recipe instead of the milk.

✽ My favourite warm, easy dessert is to combine 1¼ cups self-raising flour, 3/4 cup sugar, 120g melted butter, 1 tsp vanilla and 2 eggs. Place in a greased 24cm cake tin and top with your favourite seasonal fruits - apple, berries, even bananas or feijoa slices. Sprinkle top with 2 tblsp sugar and bake at 180°C for 1 hour. You need about 4-5 cups sliced fruit.

unusual finales

Instead of feeling pressure to serve a rich, creamy dessert torte, keep things simple for the finale. Often a fruit bowl and three favourite cheeses makes great sense. Many home cooks think extra preparation, greater expenditure of time, energy, money and fuss equates with a grand finale. You think that fancy dessert tower of profiteroles oozing with custard cream centres (the classic croquembouche), complete with hand-piped chocolate or caramel and decorated with gold leaf or spun sugar, is far better than serving a perfectly ripe pear and slice of room-temperature, gooey blue cheese – but this is far from the truth.

Give me poached fruits over tiramisu or cheesecake, simple fruit and cheese over caramel cream sponge creations any day. Feel confident serving simple, fresh, great tasting food – rather than slaving for hours in the kitchen.

While it's simple, it still has to be the best you can find – and there is much more to a stunning cheese course than a hunk of cheese, crackers and a few imported grapes on a paper doily with a garnish of parsley.

Take the idea – fruit and cheese – and take it up a notch. Select a good quality aged Cheddar and make superb, light cheese biscuits with the cheese. Serve the room-temperature cheese with these biscuits and a compote of dried fruits instead of dessert.

Slice a piece of Cheddar, place on top of the cheese biscuit and top with a plump apricot half or fat fig from the syrup. Eat and close your eyes. The buttery, slightly crunchy, savoury notes of the biscuit combined with the sturdy, full flavour of the aged cheese and topped with the contrasting intensity of the syrup-laden fruit – this is an out-of-body experience. Who needs cream cake or mousse?

CHEESE BISCUITS WITH DRIED FRUIT COMPOTE

This is the most sublime cheese course ever! Buttery, full-flavoured cheese biscuits served with boozy fruits and a delicious slice of aged Cheddar. Makes 24

1 cup flour
100g butter, cubed
100g aged Cheddar, grated

METHOD
Preheat the oven to 180°C. Place all the ingredients in a food processor and process until the mixture forms a ball.

Roll out dough onto a lightly floured surface to about 1/2cm thick, cut with a small round cutter and bake on a lightly greased tray for approximately 15 minutes.

DRIED FRUIT COMPOTE
Serves 4–6

1 cup dried apricots
1 cup dried figs
1 cup dried giant sultanas
1/2 cup boiling water
1/2 cup port
1 cup water
1 cup sugar

METHOD
Soak the fruits overnight in boiling water and port. The next day put fruits as well as liquids into a generous pot. Add the cup of water and sugar and bring to the boil. Simmer for about 10 minutes. Leave to cool and keep in the fridge.

✳ Serve in a bowl with a pile of cheese biscuits and a wedge of room-temperature aged Cheddar.

THE CHEESE FILE

✳ Always serve cheese at room temperature and if you go to buy cheese on a Saturday morning for a party that night, at this time of the year, leave it out of the fridge in a cooler part of the house. If you forget, a few minutes for a brie near a warm fire (like a bottle of opened red) will do wonders for the taste on a very cold evening.

✳ Try to buy just enough cheese for your needs as required. Once cut into, use cheese as quickly as possible and remove it from the plastic wrappers, otherwise it will deteriorate quickly. Cheese wrapped in greaseproof and stored in an airtight container in the fridge works well for a few days after it has been opened.

✳ Try a slice of creamy blue cheese with a glass of botrytis wine. Sip the wine, taste the cheese, try the wine again – magic in your mouth.

✳ Make your favourite fruit loaf or fruit bread and serve sliced with a ripe, room-temperature Brie and a small cluster of grapes. To make a delicious walnut and raisin loaf, place 1/3 cup raisins, 90g butter, 1/2 cup brown sugar and 1/3 cup water in a large saucepan and bring to the boil. Remove from heat and add 1/2 tsp baking soda and cool. Stir in 2 eggs, 1/2 cup chopped walnuts, 1/2 cup flour and 1/2 cup self-raising flour and place in a buttered and lined loaf tin. Bake for 45 minutes in a 150°C oven. Best made a day ahead of using.

✳ Serve a trio of cheeses with a slice of panforte, which is available at good bakeries and delis. It's an Italian sweet cake full of fruit, nuts and sometimes chocolate. Try a blue cheese such as the Italian-style creamy blue Gorgonzola, a wedge of Parmigiano-Reggiano and an aged Cheddar. Don't garnish the cheese platter, just serve the wedges with the panforte and a knife and fork on a simple white plate.

✳ Quince paste – available in delis and good food stores – is superb with cheese and crackers or toasted sourdough bread croutes. Next autumn, try poached quinces served with a good quality sheep's milk cheese.

✳ For fun, next summer combine cubes of feta cheese with watermelon and dust with a little cinnamon. Delicious as part of your next barbecue salad selection.

✳ Try serving a small mound of ricotta (Italian soft cheese – looks like cottage cheese) with slices of fresh fruit – use peaches, apricots or nectarines. Serve with pistachio-currant biscotti. Ricotta is available nationwide in supermarkets.

✳ Make mini apple galettes or apple tarts and serve warm with a slice of aged Cheddar. For a super-simple apple tart – buy some pre-rolled puff pastry and cut into circles, top with thin apple slices and a sprinkling of raw sugar and bake in a hot fan-bake oven until the apple is soft and pastry golden.

✳ Honey-roasted pears are delicious with a creamy blue cheese. Select firm, not-yet-ripe pears and place them, peeled, halved and cored (rub with lemon juice to prevent browning) in a baking dish with white wine (for 2 pears or 4 halves – you will need about 1/4 cup), 2 tblsp honey, 1–2 tblsp butter and a pinch of coarse black pepper. Cover and bake for 15–30 minutes until pears are tender but not overcooked. Cooking time will depend on ripeness and size of pears. Serve pears warm, not hot – you can reduce down the syrup left in the baking dish if desired and drizzle over pears on the platter with the cheese.

✳ Oven-roasted walnuts combined with honey make a delicious accompaniment to a soft, young goat's cheese. If you think roasted walnuts have a bitter taste (from the tannin in the walnuts), you can place them in a small bowl, cover with boiling water and leave for 30 minutes. Drain, pat dry and roast in a low oven (100°C) between triple thickness of paper towels for 15 minutes until completely dry.

To test the ripeness of cheese – 'You put your left index finger on your eye and your right index finger on the cheese. If they sort of feel the same, the cheese is ready.' M.TAITTINGER

One of my personal favourite baked goods is this irresistible gingerbread – a couple of warm pieces topped with baked fruits or dried fruit compote with a side dollop of cream or yoghurt. Even grilled pineapple or apricots on the barbecue are enhanced with an association with gingerbread.

THE GINGER FILE

* Make sure your ground ginger is fresh and don't be timid about the quantity of ginger used – instead of 2 tsps (see recipe) why not go for a generous tablespoon and enjoy the extra spice? Also you cannot substitute the golden syrup – it's critical for this recipe and the amount is not a misprint.

* Pears have a natural affinity with ginger, so serve wedges of the gingerbread with baked pears. To bake pears, remove the rind thinly from 1/2 lemon, avoiding the white pith. Squeeze the lemon. Combine the rind, juice, 4 pears, peeled and quartered, 1 cup caster sugar, 3 cups water and 1 bay leaf (fresh is ideal) in an ovenproof dish. Cover and bake at 180°C for 30–60 minutes depending on how firm the pears are – the firmer the pear the longer it needs to cook. You want the pears tender but not falling to pieces. Cool in syrup for extra flavour.

* Mascarpone cream is also delicious with gingerbread – and the pears as well! Place 250g mascarpone in a bowl and gently stir in 1 tsp vanilla and 1/3 cup (80ml) of the pear syrup or whatever fruit juice or cooked fruit syrup you have on hand.

* Make a trifle using gingerbread and canned drained pears for something different – adding finely minced crystallised ginger to the whipped cream would be an extra treat.

* Caramelise slices of gingerbread for even greater flavour. Cut the cooled gingerbread into 2cm thick slices, spread both sides of the gingerbread with softened butter and sprinkle with caster sugar. Cook the gingerbread in a preheated frypan (not too hot) in batches, until the sugar caramelises. Turn and repeat on the other side. Top with fruit and cream.

* Before the tamarillos disappear off the trees – serve them with other fruits in a baked fruit salad that is the perfect accompaniment to the gingerbread. Lay 3 tamarillos (peeled and sliced) on the bottom of a heatproof casserole or baking dish. Layer 1 cup dried apricots (sliced), 1/2 cup currants, 3 very firm pears (peeled and sliced), 2 plums (sliced and stones removed) and lastly 3 oranges (peeled and sliced). Drizzle over 3/4 cup brandy and 1/2 cup brown sugar. Cover and bake in a slow oven (140–150°C) for 45 minutes.

THE BEST GINGERBREAD

125g soft butter
3/4 cup (150g) firmly packed brown sugar
1 egg
13/4 cups (260g) flour
2 tsp ground cinnamon
2 tsp ground ginger
11/4 tsp baking soda
2/3 cup golden syrup
2/3 cup boiling water

METHOD

Preheat the oven to 180°C. Grease a loaf tin and line with baking paper for easy removal. Beat the butter and brown sugar in a small bowl with an electric mixer until light and fluffy. Add the egg and beat until combined. Transfer the mixture to a large bowl. Stir in the sifted dry ingredients and combined syrup and water in two batches until combined.

Pour the mixture into the prepared loaf tin and bake for 40–50 minutes. Check after 40 minutes although it usually requires longer. You can tell when the gingerbread is cooked as a skewer or sharp knife will come out cleanly from the pan.

* Better made the day before you want to use it. Will keep well for 3–5 days if stored in an airtight container. The loaf actually improves with age and freezes well.

SEPTEMBER ... whitebaiting and Keri Hulme

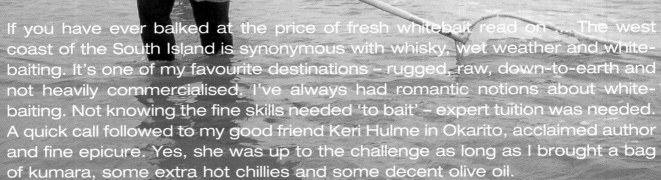

If you have ever balked at the price of fresh whitebait read on .... The west coast of the South Island is synonymous with whisky, wet weather and white-baiting. It's one of my favourite destinations – rugged, raw, down-to-earth and not heavily commercialised. I've always had romantic notions about white-baiting. Not knowing the fine skills needed 'to bait' – expert tuition was needed. A quick call followed to my good friend Keri Hulme in Okarito, acclaimed author and fine epicure. Yes, she was up to the challenge as long as I brought a bag of kumara, some extra hot chillies and some decent olive oil.

Laden with my provisions, it was simply a matter of a flight to Christchurch, a small plane ride to Hokitika, then a two-hour drive south to Okarito, population twenty-seven.

Sitting on Keri's sun-drenched porch outside her octagonal room looking out to sea, she enthused about the delights of whitebaiting and references to food in her novels. 'I'm obsessional about good food – that's why I write about it so much. It is one of our greatest pleasures and when you write about it you can recreate perfection – you can't do that in real life. It's a form of escapism perhaps?'

Whitebaiting is a great panacea, she says. Like all forms of fishing it is an atavistic activity – echoing our pre-human beginnings in the ocean, and the ancestral pleasure of catching your own food and being in control of what and how you eat. Keri feels strongly about what she consumes. In 1976 she made the 'moral decision' not to eat meat from an abattoir, only game.

Three hours had passed and my wellies had not yet been used. Could I ask her to accompany me for a few hours down by the river, to go baiting? 'River?' she queried. 'No, we go out to the edge of the lagoon right where the sea comes in. We use one of these – pointing to a large mesh strainer sitting on the porch – it's hard work.'

Images of a languid afternoon on the banks of the river, sipping a fine single malt after throwing in a net, quickly disappeared.

We set off down to the beach. It was 5.30 p.m. and the incoming tide full of bait needed to be harvested. Keri likes to go baiting every day in season, and in a good season she can gather up to 30 kilos, enjoying the whitebait best fresh but also freezing for later use.

'There is only one other stupid person out here,' she said with a laugh and pointing to one distant whitebaiter. She then proceeded to instruct me on the art of baiting. First, the

wellies were not a good idea. After nearly drowning as the water surged into my boots, I realised why her diving boots were much more practical.

'Now, it's customary to throw your first catch back into the sea,' said Keri. 'No problem,' I enthused as I threw back my first catch – only about ten bait. Meagre for sure, but I was focused on gathering 'puddings' (large catches of bait) for friends and family back at home who had pre-ordered fritters for Sunday supper.

With the setting sun, a deep azure sky and the trickle of evening smoke from wood-burning ranges painting the sky, we powered on. Keri was an expert – no sign of rising damp on her gear or unnecessary struggles with her net in the water.

For one and a half hours we sifted through the waves – it was exhausting work and I caught nine whitebait. Not nine kilos or nine puddings, but nine single whitebait – not even enough for one fritter!

On the way back to Auckland I stopped at the local pub and bought frozen bait to fill my little chilly bin for the trip north. I wanted to put a few bait in my hair, wear my wellies and pull out the Swanndri to look like a real whitebaiter, but after my abysmal efforts this seemed pretentious.

After our baiting Keri offered to cook me dinner. My nine whitebait would be stir-fried in a little butter and served on toasted wholemeal bread. A superb treatment for super-fresh bait.

Frozen bait came out of the freezer to make a few over-stuffed fritters served with lashings of white wine and a bowl of roasted kumara and peas. Keri loves Nelson scallops and some were gently poached in stock with peppercorns – stellar flavours.

KERI'S CRÊPES MALONEY
This is one of Keri's favourite meals!

Make your crêpes to your favourite recipe, but they should be unsugared and the thinner the better. For every crêpe have available 100g of bait (in emergencies, this can be reduced to 50g), 20g butter, 1 tblsp of finely chopped coriander or parsley (must be fresh), a squit (yes, that is squit – the sort of dribblet that the pepper-timid let slip out of the bottle) or a slop or a largish slurp of (this is the secret ingredient) jalapeno sauce and salt according to taste (sprinkle on the bait at the last moment prior to cooking).

Stir-fry the bait in the fizzing butter for approximately 3 minutes. Add the coriander (or the parsley), the jalapeno sauce and salt and cook for another minute. Tong out onto the waiting crêpes and roll 'em up. Pour remaining herbed-peppered butter over crêpes. (Curiously, the pepper sauce and the coriander enhance the taste of the fresh whitebait, rather than kill it.) These are very filling.

SATAY CHICKEN MARINADE

10 cloves shallots
6 cloves garlic
2.5cm fresh ginger
1 tblsp turmeric powder
7cm galangal
1kg chicken meat in cubes (bite size)
2 tblsp sugar
1 tsp salt

METHOD
Purée shallots, garlic, ginger, turmeric and galangal in a food processor. This is a dry mix, but you can add a little water if desired. Add the sugar and salt. Coat the chicken with the paste and let sit in this mix for at least 1 hour, then skewer the meat onto bamboo skewers. Grill over charcoal or gas barbecue.

✱ Substitute some of the regular sugar with palm sugar for even better results.

✱ Galangal looks like miniature horseradish and/or ginger and is available fresh at Auckland's Avondale Market, or dried from some speciality food stores and Asian and Indian supply stores. Soak dried galangal in boiling water for 20–30 minutes before use. Thailand exports water-packed jars of sliced galangal, which I prefer over dried. If you use the galangal powder (otherwise known as Laos powder) use 1 tsp of the powder instead of 4cm of fresh galangal. Ground galangal is also delicious in carrot cake, banana bread and chutneys; it is also a great replacement for ground ginger in any recipe.

✱ When cooking your satay over the barbecue coal fire, brush the meat with oil with a home-made lemon grass 'brush' for extra delicious flavour.

✱ Remember, if you are using bamboo skewers pre-soak them first, otherwise they will burn.

BACON BURGERS
Makes 4 burgers

Home-made bacon burgers are simply irresistible, so enjoy these delicious, simple-to-prepare, family favourites.

400g lean beef mince
6–8 rashers lean bacon
2–3 cloves garlic, minced
salt and freshly ground black pepper
2 tblsp Thai sweet chilli sauce
2 spring onions, chopped
1 egg

slices of blue cheese (optional)
mayonnaise to spread on rolls
2–3 tomatoes, sliced
1/2 avocado, sliced
salad greens
4 hamburger bread rolls

METHOD
In a bowl combine the mince, 2–3 rashers of diced bacon, garlic, seasoning, chilli sauce, spring onions and egg. Form into patties and grill in a hot frypan or on a hot grill for 2–4 minutes on each side. If desired, in the last minute or two of cooking, place a few slices of blue vein cheese on top of the burger and allow to melt. Meanwhile, cook remaining bacon. Place burger and rasher of bacon in a bread roll smeared with mayonnaise. Top with sliced tomatoes, avocado and salad greens.

SUMMER SALAD WITH ROSEMARY
Orzo is a barley-shaped pasta available from speciality food stores. It looks like rice, and will have your guests fooled. Serves 4

250g orzo pasta
1½ cup pinenuts, toasted
1 cup feta cheese
2 cloves garlic, minced
¼ cup fresh rosemary
¼ cup olive oil
juice from 1 lemon
1 cup olives

METHOD
Cook orzo in boiling water according to directions on the packet, being careful not to overcook. Drain and rinse in cold water. Lightly brown pinenuts in a dry pan. Set aside to cool. Crumble the cheese over pasta. Mix garlic and rosemary and lightly toss all ingredients together, except olives. Refrigerate until ready to serve. Then either put a few olives on each serving plate or surround salad bowl with them.

✱ Another delicious suggestion is to add blanched snow peas and pieces of warm, cooked fresh salmon. A great way to cook a side of fresh salmon is to remove the bones and place in double tinfoil. In a jar with a secure lid place 6 tblsp brown sugar, 8 tsp Dijon mustard, 2 tblsp soy sauce and 2 tsp rice vinegar. Shake well, then pour over salmon and secure the foil well. Leave for 30 minutes on a cool bench, then cook until medium rare on a hot barbecue. It will only take 6–8 minutes, depending on the heat of your grill.

CORNED BEEF HASH

This great American classic was formerly an excellent way of using up leftovers after a Yankee corned beef boiled dinner. It uses leftover corned beef and potatoes, and is irresistible for breakfast with eggs and slices of grilled bacon. This can easily be made on the hot plate of the barbecue, or use a frypan over the grill.

3 tblsp olive oil
1 cup chopped onions
1/2 medium green capsicum, chopped
2–3 tsp fresh thyme
3 cups cubed corned beef
2–3 cups leftover cooked potatoes (cubed)
salt and freshly ground black pepper to season
poached or fried eggs and grilled bacon to serve
additional fresh thyme for garnish

METHOD

In a large frypan heat the oil and add the onions, capsicum and thyme. Cook for 3–4 minutes on medium heat, stirring, until lightly coloured. Add the corned beef and potatoes, stir once and reduce the heat. Press down with a spatula to compress the hash. Cook for 10–15 minutes without disturbing until the bottom is well-browned. Slide or invert the hash onto a serving plate. Serve with eggs and grilled bacon. Garnish with thyme.

✱ Try this with a little Thai sweet chilli sauce on the side!

BARBECUED BANANAS

Everyone has a favourite way to cook bananas on the barbecue. Every way is delicious with a scoop of vanilla ice-cream!

4 bananas
2–3 tblsp butter, softened
4 tblsp brown sugar
4 tsp orange rind
2 tblsp rum or orange juice
cream or plain yoghurt for
 garnish

METHOD

Place the bananas in their skins on the hot barbecue and leave for 6–8 minutes, turning occasionally, until they turn brownish-black in colour. Mix the butter, brown sugar, orange rind and orange juice or rum together and reserve.

Place the cooked bananas (still in their skins) into individual dessert bowls. Using a sharp knife, slit the skin and open out enough to add a little of the flavoured butter.

Serve immediately.

* You can also make banana parcels with a peeled banana and the above ingredients placed in a tinfoil parcel – cook for a few minutes only.

TWO-MUSTARD VINAIGRETTE

Delicious to drizzle over chargrilled vegetables and crumbled feta! Makes 1 cup

1 tblsp Dijon mustard
1 tblsp wholegrain mustard
2 tsp sherry vinegar
1 tsp sea salt
1 cup olive oil
freshly ground black pepper

METHOD

In a small bowl mix mustards, vinegar and salt.

Slowly whisk in the olive oil to create a smooth, creamy emulsion. Add pepper to taste.

The vinaigrette can be stored for up to 2 weeks, refrigerated, in a jar with a tight-fitting lid.

Whisk before serving.

* If the dressing has been sitting in the fridge for a while, jazz it up by adding a squirt of fresh lemon or orange juice. This completely revitalises a salad dressing!

GINGER VINAIGRETTE

Delicious as a dipping sauce with fresh seafood, either raw, for example, with oysters, or use to drizzle over chargrilled fish, pork or chicken. Makes 11/4 cups

1 tblsp grated fresh ginger
1 tblsp Dijon mustard
1 tsp powdered mustard
1 tblsp soy sauce
grated zest and juice of 1 small
 lime
2 tsp rice vinegar
1 cup extra virgin olive oil

METHOD

In a small bowl mix ginger, Dijon mustard, powdered mustard, soy sauce, lime zest and juice and rice vinegar.

Slowly whisk in olive oil to create a smooth creamy emulsion. The vinaigrette can be stored for up to 2 weeks, refrigerated, in a jar with a tight-fitting lid. Whisk before serving.

BBQ SUGGESTIONS

* Remember, gentlemen, 'no poking, no pricking and only one turn' when it comes to a steak on the grill. Try to cook your steaks less and leave time for them to rest before serving. Always start your cooking with room-temperature meat.

* For your next barbecue, combine 3 tblsp balsamic vinegar, 2 cloves garlic (crushed), 2 tblsp olive oil and cracked pepper and throw in 4 chicken breast fillets. Marinate for 5 minutes, then sizzle on the barbecue for a few minutes on a hot grill. Turn only once and serve with chargrilled lime halves.

* Combine 3-4 tblsp char siu sauce with equal amounts of hoisin sauce and a few tsps of sesame oil for the simplest and most delicious marinade for chicken breasts. Cook on the grill as per normal.

* A co-worker of mine, Yvonne, swears by mixing 1 tablespoon grainy mustard with 2 tblsp balsamic vinegar, 2 tsp minced garlic and 2 tblsp oil and marinating the chicken in that mix for 15–30 minutes. Throw it on the barbecue. It blackens and looks strange but tastes divine!

* Marinate Nelson scallops in sweet chilli sauce, lime juice and olive oil for a short period. Do not over-marinate scallops or you lose their natural flavour and they cook in the marinade instead. Pan-sear for 1 minute on each side — a total of 2 minutes, depending on the heat of the pan and size of the scallops.

Chargrilled vegetables topped with crumbled feta cheese and drizzled with two-mustard vinaigrette

baking

DIVINE APRICOT MUFFINS

White chocolate and a hint of jam make these extra special. We made them on television using low fat milk (to balance the use of the more indulgent ingredients!) and the results were amazing. Within seconds the crew had eaten them all and subtle hints were made about up-coming birthdays and special events where these muffins could feature!
Makes 6 large or 8 smaller muffins

13/4 cups flour
1/2 cup sugar
1 tblsp minced crystallised ginger (optional)
11/2 tsp baking powder
1/2 tsp salt
60g white baking chocolate, finely chopped
3/4 cup milk
3 tblsp butter, melted
1 large egg, lightly beaten
cooking spray
1/2 cup apricot jam
lemon juice and sugar to glaze (optional)

METHOD

Preheat the oven to 200°C. In a medium bowl combine flour with the next five ingredients and stir well with a whisk.

Make a well in the centre of the mixture. Combine the milk, butter and egg and stir well with a whisk. Add to the flour mixture, stirring until just moist, no more.

Spoon 1 tblsp batter into greased muffin tins, add a teaspoon of apricot jam and then top with remaining batter.

Bake at 200°C for 22 minutes or until the muffin springs back when touched lightly in the centre. Remove from the pan and drizzle the lemon juice and sugar over the top.

Cool completely before eating.

TIPS FOR BETTER BAKING

✳ When it comes to baking, accuracy in recipes is important and sometimes doubling a recipe will not work. The secret to great baking is to keep the ratio of fat, sugar and flour as given. In particular, take care with baking powder and baking soda - a heavy hand with these ingredients can be a disaster.

✳ It's important to use the same size tin as specified in the recipe. Using a smaller or bigger tin will alter the cooking times. Always check to ensure a cake is cooked by using a cake tester (a very thin metal skewer). Insert it into the middle of the cake and if it withdraws clean, the cake is cooked.

✳ Have eggs at room temperature for better volume, not cold from the refrigerator. However, eggs are more stable when straight from the fridge, so for separating - as in pavlova or meringues - do so when cold.

✳ Use the fan-bake option on your stove for baking biscuits and muffins, but if you can, use regular bake for your cakes.

✳ Even if you use a mixer for creaming, always stir in or fold in the flour gently by hand. Mixing cake batters too vigorously will work up the gluten (proteins) in the flour and result in a tough cake. Conversely, working the gluten is exactly what's required when making bread - hence the necessity for kneading dough.

✳ A cake mixer takes the chore out of creaming butter and sugar, but ensure your butter is properly softened first. You can also cream butter and sugar by hand in a medium-sized bowl using a wooden spoon or in a food processor. If using a food processor, the butter should be cool-to-room temperature and not completely soft as the action of the processor can cause very soft butter to turn oily.

✳ Select cake tins with strong construction and well-sealed seams. It isn't necessary to use non-stick bakeware if you grease and flour the tin or line it with baking paper before using it.

✳ A wire cooling rack is essential baking equipment - place the cake, biscuits or bread straight on it and allow to cool either in or out of the tin, on or off the tray, according to the recipe directions. Using a rack ensures air circulation and helps with even cooling.

CITRUS YOYOS

Take an old-fashioned tried and true recipe like the one found in our classic *Edmonds Cookbook* and add your own personal flavour. Great zingy, buttery flavour is achieved here with citrus added in both the delicate biscuit as well as the filling. Invite a friend over for 'a cup of tea and sympathy' and whip these up for a special treat. One of life's greatest pleasures is a well-laden afternoon tea tray!

175g butter
1/2 cup icing sugar
few drops vanilla essence
2 tsp finely grated lemon zest
11/2 cups flour
1/4 cup custard powder

BUTTER ICING
50g butter, softened
1/2 cup icing sugar
2 tblsp custard powder
1–2 tsp lemon juice
1 tsp lemon zest

METHOD
Cream the butter and icing sugar until light and fluffy. Add vanilla and lemon zest. Sift flour and custard powder together. Mix sifted ingredients into creamed mixture. Roll a teaspoonful of mixture into balls and place onto a greased oven tray. Flatten with a fork. Bake at 180°C for 15–20 minutes. When cold, sandwich together in twos with butter icing.

BUTTER ICING
Beat all the ingredients together until well combined.

celebration of green

Asparagus joyously heralds spring and warmer days ahead, along with casual buckets of spring flowers at the dairy and increasing daylight

Asparagus is a vegetable well worth celebrating. It is easy to prepare and loves an association with the simplest foods – eggs, Parmesan cheese, or simply lemon juice, butter and black pepper – but there is so much more to this tender spring shoot. Steam or chargrill on the barbecue and serve with an anchovy mayonnaise, or go Asian and whip up a wasabi variation. It can handle powerful and intense salty flavours such as prosciutto, yet delicately seasons a scallop or prawn stir-fry. Speaking of seafood – try just-cooked asparagus with crab and either orange or sweet grapefruit salad. The sweetness of the seafood, the citrus zing and that herbaceous quality of the fresh asparagus is a total palate pleaser.

Fresh asparagus can be blanched in hot water for a few minutes and then added to omelettes, to a favourite pizza as a topping, to an antipasto platter with a dipping sauce of balsamic vinegar or cut into manageable pieces for a pasta or risotto.

If you enjoy the comforts of a vegetable pie or quiche, or even cheese on toast, try fresh asparagus as an important ingredient. Gruyère cheese and asparagus make for a sensational flavour partnership; the nutty flavour of this

❋ Asparagus spears are delicious roasted – wonderful with chopped capsicums, haloumi cheese, peeled tomatoes, garlic and olive oil, cooked until just charred and served with lots of crusty bread to soak up the juices.

❋ Serve cooked asparagus with a simple dressing. Don't waste your money on bottles of ready-made dressing; much better ones can be made, very simply, at home. You will need a good olive oil, wine vinegar or citrus juice, Dijon mustard, chopped herbs and seasoning. In a bowl mix all the ingredients, except the oil, which you add a small splash at a time, until you reach the tanginess you like. Store in a bottle or jar and shake well before serving. For extra panache – add orange segments to the salad, and orange juice to the dressing, and sprinkle with chopped roasted hazelnuts.

❋ For a superb dinner party treat serve just-cooked salmon fillet with roasted asparagus and a lemon-caper sauce. Combine 2 tblsp fresh lemon juice, 2 tblsp minced red onion, 1 tblsp olive oil, 1 tblsp chopped drained capers, 1 tsp chopped fresh thyme, 1/2 tsp grated lemon peel and drizzle over the hot asparagus.

❋ Make your favourite quiche or vegetable tart and add slices of Gruyère cheese and blanched asparagus. Serve with a mixed green salad and a basket of French bread.

❋ Serve chargrilled asparagus with creamy blue cheese butter. Combine 3/4 cup crumbled creamy blue cheese (loosely packed) and 6 tblsp (85g) softened butter

with a squeeze of lemon juice. Cover and refrigerate – can be made 2 days ahead. Asparagus is equally delicious with Parmesan butter.

❋ Serve roasted asparagus with goats' cheese and bacon. Grill asparagus lightly coated with olive oil, place on platter, and while still warm sprinkle goats' cheese over the asparagus and the slices of warm cooked bacon. Garnish with a hint of lemon peel and a squeeze of fresh lemon juice.

❋ Add just-cooked asparagus to a new potato salad and drizzle with a herbed vinaigrette.

❋ Use the leftover stalks for flavouring soups or stocks.

❋ Serve just-cooked asparagus on a piece of hot sourdough or wholemeal toast with butter and salt and pepper.

❋ I like to add just-cooked asparagus to salads with Gruyère cheese, red onion, salad greens and chopped ham. Just drizzle a little herb mustard vinaigrette over the top and enjoy with crusty bread.

❋ Freshly cooked asparagus can be topped with shavings of fresh Parmesan and grilled in the oven – sublime.

❋ Asparagus is delicious in a stir-fry, just add crushed garlic to a heated wok with oil. Add blanched asparagus pieces, cook for a minute and add a generous slurp of soy sauce, a pinch of brown sugar, one or two tablespoonfuls of sesame oil and top it all off with a few teaspoonfuls of sesame seeds.

CHARGRILLED ASPARAGUS WITH CORN SALSA

Asparagus and egg create a classic marriage of flavours. Add the texture and natural sweetness of corn and capsicum and you have both great flavours as well as an eye-catching dish. Serves 4

3 eggs
2 tblsp milk
1 tblsp olive oil
2 cobs corn (we used the corn in the sealed packs)
1 small red onion, diced
1 red capsicum, finely chopped
2 tblsp chopped fresh thyme
2 tblsp olive oil, extra
2 tblsp balsamic vinegar
24 fresh asparagus spears
1 tblsp walnut or macadamia oil
toasted wholegrain bread

METHOD
Beat the eggs and milk to combine. Heat the oil in a non-stick frypan, add the egg and cook over a medium heat until just set. Flip and cook the other side. Remove and allow to cool, then roll up and cut into thick slices. Cook the corn on a chargrill or in boiling water until tender. Set aside to cool slightly, then slice off the corn kernels. Make the salsa by gently combining the corn, onion, capsicum, thyme, olive oil and balsamic vinegar. Trim off woody ends from the asparagus, lightly brush with your favourite flavoured oil and cook on the chargrill until tender. Serve the asparagus topped with a little salsa and sliced egg, accompanied by fingers of buttered toast.

cheese also explains why asparagus and hazelnuts work in harmony.

Asparagus is versatile, fun, easy-to-prepare and can be served just as an entrée for lunch with a poached egg, gratings of fresh Parmesan and a good grinding of black pepper. Even if your samplers say they don't like asparagus – based on experiences with canned variations and scary encounters with asparagus rolls in their youth – encourage them to go for the fresh young spears instead.

To prepare asparagus, wash and bend the spear until it snaps off at the woody end – those woody ends can be used in your next stock for flavour. Chefs argue you should always peel asparagus, but to me that is just creating too much work for casual, family dinners – just try to select firm, young, thin spears and there is no excessive stringiness.

Labour weekend brings a flurry of activity in the garden and is the time to delight in full spring fare. The barbecue is cleaned down, the tomato plants placed in the garden and fresh asparagus and broad beans are celebrated.

Broad beans (also known as fava beans) just radiate spring and early summer, and this is the best time to enjoy them. Many cooks don't know what to do with them – they look like overgrown runner beans and inside have shells like peas. So simply open them up and do very little to them – they are simply delicious and love an association with bacon and fresh rosemary or sage. Many recipes do suggest eating them raw, either with olive oil, sea salt and shavings of Parmesan cheese or in a salad with other Mediterranean ingredients, but I would recommend cooking them as some people react quite violently to uncooked broad beans. Seriously speaking though, people of Greek and Armenian ancestry are more prone to an inherited allergy to toxins found in raw broad beans.

Shell the beans (try to select smaller pods, the beans are smaller, but a more delicate flavour) and cook for 3 minutes in boiling water. Drain quickly under cold water, so that the beans can be handled, and then slip each bean out of its tough skin.

Not all cooks remove the skin – certainly this is not necessary on small delicate beans. It's a matter of choice.

✳ Try a great broad bean salad idea – serve just-cooked broad beans with feta, chopped olives and mint, tossed in a vinaigrette.

✳ My favourite way of eating broad beans is simply to shell, blanch, remove the skin and serve heated through again with a little butter, fresh herbs, a pinch of sea salt and pepper. Guard the bowl, such a labour of love should not be scoffed by the unappreciative!

✳ If you grow your own supply then freeze the beans – they behave well after freezing. The tops of the plants can be eaten cooked, as one does spinach.

✳ Traditionally, broad beans were always served with hot boiled bacon and parsley sauce. Try your broad beans with slices of ham and new potatoes and serve a light parsley sauce on the side.

✳ Try combining freshly cooked broad beans with finely sliced, raw mushrooms. Toss in your favourite vinaigrette and add some finely chopped chives or spring onions and chopped parsley.

✳ Another salad suggestion – place quickly cooked broad beans in a bowl with thin orange slices, sliced radishes, sliced cucumber and diced feta cheese. Toss a herb vinaigrette through and season with pepper.

✳ Cooked and shelled broad beans can be puréed with a little garlic and cream or crème fraîche in your food processor. Just add a touch of little horseradish to the mix for extra flavour delights. For 500g broad beans – try 2 tsp horseradish and add more if desired. Serve hot – reheating in the microwave is easy.

✳ Another broad bean purée suggestion is to combine in the food processor 1kg cooked, shelled broad beans with 1/2 cup of the bean cooking water, 2 cloves garlic, 1 tsp freshly chopped oregano, 1 tsp ground cumin, 150ml olive oil and salt and pepper. Serve with toasted pita bread slices.

BROAD BEANS TOSSED WITH FRESH HERBS AND BACON
Serves 4

50g butter
1 tblsp olive oil
1 medium onion, sliced
8 strips bacon slices
1 tsp chopped garlic
4 cups broad beans, blanched and skins removed
3 tblsp fresh herbs, chopped

METHOD
Heat butter and olive oil in a frypan and sauté sliced onion, bacon and garlic. When cooked (approximately 2 minutes) add blanched beans and fresh herbs.

✳ Skins on or off is a matter of choice – if you have the time and depending on the size of the beans – you can go with either.

Spinach is not everyone's first choice of vegetable. Blame it on those unpleasant experiences as a child when 'another mouthful for Popeye' left a funny aftertaste in your mouth. This was partly due to the cooking method and also more importantly because our youthful taste-buds couldn't handle it. Our palates definitely change over the years. We all know that as we get older our preference for savoury over sweet flavours becomes more prevalent, and at a young age our taste-buds do react differently: for a five-year-old child the taste of eating cooked cabbage is similar to an adult's taste of eating sauerkraut. Spinach, like cabbage, improves in flavour as we mature.

Spring screams spinach. Vibrant green, full of goodness and so versatile – this cluster of green leaves in the garden is a personal favourite. If you have been put off spinach before then get brave and try the deliciously delicate baby spinach leaves available at your greengrocer or supermarket in your next salad and you will be delighted.

We have our own variety of spinach in New Zealand, known internationally as New Zealand spinach. It has flat, spade-shaped leaves, a bulkier flavour and thrives in hotter weather.

SPINACH AND FETA FRITTERS

These spinach and feta fritters are simply delicious fresh from the pan. Stack with smoked salmon and top with a dollop of crème fraîche or sour cream and you have a feast of colour and flavour. **Serves 4**

3 cups fresh spinach
3 spring onions, finely chopped
2 tblsp finely chopped mint
1–2 cloves garlic, minced
2 tblsp finely chopped parsley
200g feta, crumbled
freshly ground black pepper
4 eggs, beaten
1/2 cup flour
1 tsp baking powder
olive oil for frying
slices of smoked salmon and sour
 cream or crème fraîche to serve

METHOD
Finely chop the spinach. Place all the remaining ingredients (except the olive oil for frying and salmon) in a large bowl and whisk together. Add the spinach and combine. Check seasoning. In a pan of hot oil add the fritters and cook until golden on one side and then the other.

Serve with a dollop of sour cream and slices of smoked salmon.

* The spinach is finely sliced so it doesn't need precooking or wilting for this recipe – you just add it raw.

'Spinach: Divide into little piles. Rearrange again into new piles. After five or six manoeuvres, sit back and say you are full.' DELIA EPHRON

THE SPINACH FILE

✳ Fresh spinach is available all year round. Choose leaves that are crisp and dark green with a nice fresh fragrance. Avoid those that are limp, damaged or have yellow spots. Refrigerate in a plastic bag for up to 3 days. Spinach must be thoroughly washed and rinsed as it is usually very gritty.

✳ Whenever you see the words 'a la Florentine' or simply 'Florentine' on a menu – for example, eggs Florentine – you know spinach is an integral ingredient in the dish.

* Wilting spinach is very easy in the microwave – just wash well, shake off all excess water and place in a glass bowl with plastic wrap over. After a few minutes in the microwave the spinach will have wilted; drain the juice off. If you do not have a microwave – cook spinach by placing the washed leaves, with only the water that remains on the leaves, in a tightly covered stainless-steel pan and heat gently. Drain (always keep that water for soups, sauces and stocks) and roughly chop, then season to taste.

* The next time you are making jazzed-up mashed potatoes, add spinach and cheese. Just mash Agria or your favourite floury potato and add wilted and drained spinach with a generous handful of Gruyère cheese. Season well. Remember to add warm milk for even creamier results with your mashed potato and serve this great mash with chargrilled chicken or other meat. The secret is to ensure that all the liquid from the cooked spinach is drained from the spinach before adding to the mashed potatoes.

* For your next spinach salad combine baby spinach leaves, halved cherry tomatoes, grilled bacon, avocado slices and hard-boiled eggs. Drizzle with a Dijon dressing – take the juice of 1 lemon, 1 tblsp white wine vinegar, 1 generous tsp Dijon mustard, 1/4 cup vegetable oil, 1 tsp sugar, sea salt and pepper to taste and shake well in an airtight jar.

* Don't forget spinach at breakfast. One of my favourite breakfast combinations is Eggs Benedict, but instead of ham and poached eggs with hollandaise sauce try smoked salmon on wilted spinach on a toasted English muffin with a hollandaise sauce with a hint of wholegrain mustard. Sensational! Also try smoked fish kedgeree with baby spinach leaves added at the last minute of cooking. Top with poached eggs and chives – a real winner for brunch.

* If you have a favourite savoury cheese pudding – try adding cubes of ham and spinach leaves over the bread cubes or slices. It looks great and adds so much more flavour.

* Spinach combined with raisins and pinenuts is a classic Mediterranean side dish to accompany delicate fish or poultry dishes and is often served at room temperature. Rinse 1kg spinach well and remove the stems. Place in a large sauté pan with only the rinsing water clinging to the leaves. Cook for a few minutes over medium heat, turning as needed until wilted. Drain well and set aside. Add 2–3 tblsp olive oil to the now-empty pan and place over medium heat. Add 6 chopped spring onions and sauté for about 8 minutes until tender. Add the spinach, 4 tblsp raisins and 4 tblsp toasted pinenuts and sauté briefly to warm through. Season with salt and pepper and serve warm or at room temperature. Serves 6.

PORK SCOTCH FILLET WRAPPED IN BACON

One of my favourite ways to celebrate spinach is to add it to a main course as part of a stuffing – delicious flavours, great colour and for those friends who can't face the idea of eating too much spinach, this is an effective way of showcasing the vegetable without any reaction, except pure delight!

150g middle bacon, diced
1/2 cup toasted pinenuts
1 tblsp grated orange rind
1/2 cup finely chopped apricots
2 cups fresh breadcrumbs
freshly ground black pepper
1 large egg yolk
1 bunch spinach, stalks removed
1.5kg pork Scotch fillet
180g middle bacon rashers

METHOD
Preheat the oven to 160°C. Cook the diced bacon and place in a large bowl with the pinenuts, orange rind, apricots, breadcrumbs, black pepper to taste and the egg yolk.

Mix well and set aside. Blanch the spinach leaves in boiling water, drain and rinse in cold water, then drain again thoroughly.

Butterfly the pork Scotch fillet by cutting down the length of the fillet, three-quarters of the way through. Open the fillet out and press flat.

Spread the spinach leaves over the cut surface of the pork. Spread the breadcrumb mixture in a log in the middle, then roll up and place the bacon strips around the pork fillet. Secure with string.

Place on a rack in a roasting tray and cook for 11/2 hours or until cooked (a meat thermometer inserted should reach 71–76°C).

Remove from the oven and stand dish, covered, in a warm place for 10 minutes.

* Make a gravy from the pan drippings and serve with oven-roasted vegetables and a salad.
* Kumara and potato mash with parsley is the perfect base. Place slices of the pork fillet on top of the mash. Make a simple sauce by reducing stock with the addition of apricot chutney or cranberry sauce and a little mustard and cook down to a suitable consistency.

beetroot

Let us praise the ruby-red beet otherwise known as the *Beta vulgaris*. For years beetroot was consigned to the pickle jar, kiwi hamburger or a last-minute addition to a cold meat lunch. Now it has become very smart and boldly struts its stuff on the most fashionable menus.

Talented chefs have boosted it up the social scale. They reduce beetroot juice down and it makes a colourful and sweet contrast for a perfectly appointed savoury meal, or they cook grated beetroot with orange, vinegar and sugar and spice and serve it as 'beetroot confit' with lamb, cervena or duck and the results are delicious.

Historically, beetroot has had some devoted fans. In 1699 John Evelyn described beetroot as a 'grateful sallet ... eaten with oyl and vinegar', and Mrs Raffald in *The Experienced English Housekeeper* (1769) has a recipe for a pink-coloured pancake which she says, 'makes a pretty corner dish for either dinner or supper'. More recently, this century beetroot has been made into fritters, au gratin, devilled and even combined with a packet of jelly to make a 1950's style moulded salad. A dish which 'rings with brave effrontery', wrote British food writer Jane Grigson of her imaginative pairing of sole with beetroot. She also described beetroot as 'the bossy vegetable' because its colour can take over the kitchen.

Beetroot fans admire and extol the versatility and sturdiness of their beloved vegetable, but generally speaking, the beetroot remains the problem child of the root vegetable world for two reasons. Firstly, if your only experience with beetroot has been via canned and sliced beetroot, you may underestimate the wonderful versatility of this humble vegetable. It can be steamed, boiled, baked or grated – eaten hot, cold or raw.

Secondly, many home cooks fear the bright seepage from the vegetable. The key is to allow 5cm of root below the base of the vegetable to remain intact. You cook the beetroot first, then remove the skin for many recipes.

So, explore the beet's interior depths and celebrate the sweetness – you may be pleasantly surprised. But remember, this is a vegetable that needs company, which is why it is so happy in a strong vinaigrette, paired with a pungent cheese, for example blue vein or feta, or sparring with an excessively tart tomato in a sauce. Beetroot can also handle outspoken herbs and spices such as dill, fennel, cumin and coriander.

* Fresh beetroot should have smooth skin, with no splitting or scars around the tops. Do not buy beetroot if the stems have been cut level with the root as the colour will start to leach as soon as it is put in water.

* To boil beetroot - allow 1½ hours for extra large beets and 30 minutes for small beets. Insert a skewer to test. The skewer should easily go right through the vegetable. You can steam the vegetables - allow an hour for large beetroot - or perhaps roast them by wrapping in foil and baking for 2 hours at 180°C.

* Yes, you can eat the young and fresh leaves - either as a steamed vegetable or thrown into pasta dishes, soups or stews.

* Combine beetroot with apple as a salad with smoked fish, and dress with a creamy horseradish dressing.

* Beetroot handles strong salty, fishy tastes well. Add anchovies to your salad dressing to accompany your warm beetroot, or a Thai salad dressing with chilli, lime juice, palm sugar (use brown if you don't have palm sugar) and fish sauce works well.

* Balsamic and sherry vinegar work well with roasted beetroot. Try baking beetroot with small red onions, then sprinkle with balsamic vinegar, lots of chopped parsley and some shavings of Parmesan.

* Beetroot cooked with red onion, tamarind, chilli and fresh coriander makes a great relish to serve with cervena or duck. Sweeten with a little brown sugar and sharpen with fresh lime juice.

* Try a beet stir-fry with walnut oil, ginger and orange juice. Remember, grating raw beetroot will cause bright seepage, but the results are worth the temporary chaos in the kitchen.

* Try a beetroot tarte tartin - take cooked beetroot, caramelise with balsamic vinegar, butter and a little sugar and bake underneath a layer of rich pastry with the addition of Parmesan cheese. Serve with crème fraîche stirred through with chopped chives.

* To make a simple beetroot salad - in a covered dish microwave for 10 minutes on high some well-scrubbed beetroot in their skins. Test with a skewer and continue cooking in 2 minute bursts until tender. Allow to cool so you can handle easily, then remove the skin and dice. While still warm toss through a coriander-inspired dressing with a hint of ginger and top with chopped chives.

* Precooked beets (1kg) can be reheated in a pan with 3 tblsp balsamic vinegar and 2 tblsp maple syrup or honey and 1 tblsp olive oil. Cook until heated through and coat well. Serve with freshly chopped thyme.

ROASTED BEETROOT, KUMARA AND BABY ONIONS

Serve this easy dish as an accompaniment to tuna or swordfish, or by itself with couscous and a yoghurt, cucumber and mint salad. **Serves 4**

5 tblsp olive oil
1 tblsp sherry vinegar, plus a little extra
2 tblsp coriander seeds, crushed
juice and minced zest of 1/2 orange
1 tblsp thyme sprigs
sea salt and freshly ground black pepper
1/2 tsp brown sugar
1 bunch small (baby) beetroot (about 450g)
250g baby (pickling) onions, peeled but left whole
3 whole chillies, halved and seeded
2 kumara (about 400g in total) peeled and cut
 into chunks
1 tsp chopped fresh thyme

METHOD

Preheat the oven to 220°C. Place the oil, vinegar, coriander seeds, juice, orange zest and thyme sprigs in a large bowl and beat together. Season with salt, pepper and the brown sugar. Trim the leaves off the beetroot and cut in halves or quarters. Toss the beetroot, onions and chillies in the oil mixture and turn into a large shallow roasting pan. Roast uncovered for 25 minutes, stirring once or twice. Add the kumara and cook again for another 35–40 minutes, stirring once. Add the chopped fresh thyme 5 minutes before the end of cooking. Sprinkle with a little sea salt and more sherry vinegar just prior to serving.

SIMPLE BEET TARTAR
Serves 6

5 medium beets, scrubbed
1 small shallot, chopped
4 tblsp chopped capers
4 tblsp chopped gherkins
1 tblsp mayonnaise
3 tblsp chopped parsley
1 tsp salt
1/2 tsp chilli sauce
1/2 tsp Worcestershire sauce

METHOD

Heat the oven to 200°C. Wrap the beets in tinfoil and roast for 1 hour, or until soft.

Peel and quarter the beets and process in a food processor until they are smaller than a small dice. Combine with the remaining ingredients.

✱ Serve at room temperature with thin toasted bread slices.

carrots

These recipes include three super simple ways of enjoying carrots. The soup is a family favourite and ideal for lunch on a cold day, served with crusty bread. The creamed carrots are delicious with everything from a roast beef or pork dinner through to an accompaniment to grilled fish or hearty lamb shanks. Try the surprise carrots with grilled chicken breasts, a salad and oven-roasted potatoes with garlic and fresh rosemary.

✴ If you want to try making some old-fashioned carrot jam, wash and grate some carrots, then boil until reduced to a thick pulp. To 500g of this pulp add 255g sugar, the juice and grated rind of 2 lemons and 85g butter or margarine. Boil the mixture well for 45 minutes to 1 hour. The result is a useful and inexpensive jam.

✴ A great idea for a snack and a healthy option for the family is to prepare some carrot sticks (as well as celery) in advance and place them in a glass of water in the fridge.

✴ If you have a juicer – try carrot juice with grated ginger. It's just delicious!

✴ For a delicious lunch serve raw carrot in very fine threads on top of cubes of Gruyère cheese and ham sitting on fresh salad greens. Make up your favourite vinaigrette and have this in a jug on the side. Serve this salad with crunchy bread. The key to raw carrot in salads is the way it is grated or prepared. Big chunks of raw carrot are difficult to eat – but grated is ideal.

CREAMED CARROTS

These are delicious by themselves but if you want to add parsnips, swedes or turnips to the pot as well, it will be a savoury delight! **Serves 4**

500g carrots
30g butter
2 tblsp cream
salt and freshly ground
 black pepper to taste
pinch nutmeg

METHOD
Scrape or thinly peel the carrots, then cut into even-sized pieces. Cook as above until tender. Strain off the water, mash well and add the butter, cream, salt and pepper and a pinch of nutmeg.

SURPRISE CARROTS

Like creamed carrots but extra savoury!

900g carrots
2 tblsp butter
1 medium onion, grated
170g grated cheese
1/2 tsp salt
1/2 tsp freshly ground
 black pepper

METHOD
Pare, slice and steam carrots, until tender. Mash carrots well then add butter, onion and cheese. Season to taste. Place the carrot mixture in a buttered casserole and bake for 40 minutes at 180°C until bubbling.

If you wish, you may add chopped green capsicum and sprinkle the top with breadcrumbs and small knobs of butter before baking. Great with chicken or lamb.

CARROT AND BASIL SOUP

2 onions, chopped
2 cloves garlic, minced
2 tsp dried basil or 11/2
 tblsp fresh basil, chopped
1kg carrots, peeled and chopped
60g butter
4 cups water
1 green capsicum, finely
 chopped
300g whole kernel corn,
 reserve corn liquid
2 tblsp flour
3 cups milk
2 tblsp sour cream (optional)
125g grated tasty
 Cheddar cheese
salt and freshly ground
 black pepper
1/3 cup chopped chives

METHOD
Sauté the onion, garlic and basil in butter for 3 minutes on a low heat. You want to soften the onions, not colour them.

Add carrots and coat in the onion/butter mix, then before they catch, add the water. Simmer for 40 minutes. Process until puréed and return to the pot. Add the capsicum, corn and corn liquid to the pot.

Mix the flour in a little milk and add to the pot along with the remaining milk.

Over moderate heat cook the soup until the capsicum is tender.

Add the sour cream (optional) and cheese and stir until combined and cheese is melted.

Season with salt and pepper and sprinkle with chopped chives.

✴ Serve with crusty bread rolls.

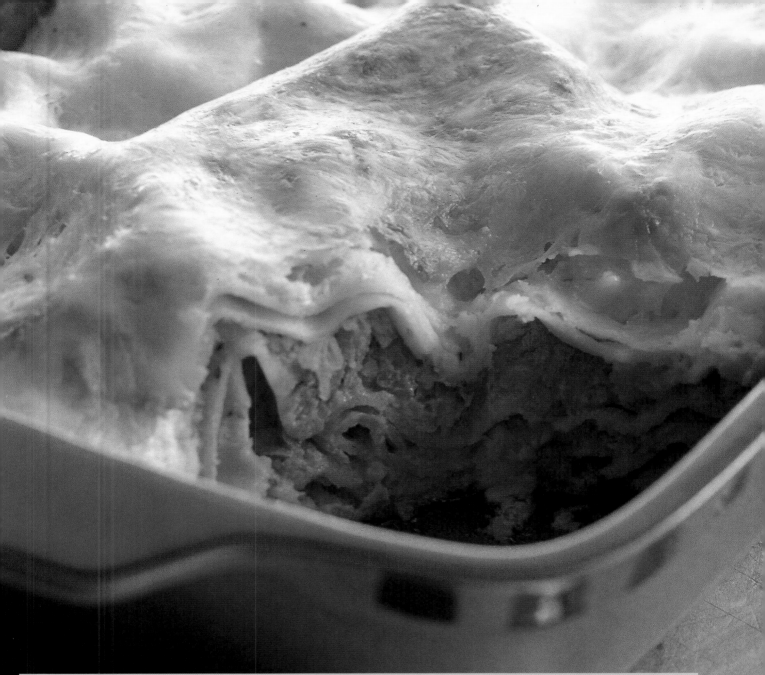

CARROT PESTO BAKE

If you are following a vegetarian diet and you want great flavour and variety, why not try this delicious carrot pesto bake – a lasagne with a difference. Instead of meat or seafood, the main attraction is the cheese and carrots with a hint of pesto.

Serves 4

50g butter
1/2 cup flour
3 cups milk
2/3 cup light sour cream
1 tsp cracked pepper
100g Edam cheese, grated
4 eggs, lightly beaten
2 tblsp pesto
750g carrots, peeled and grated
250g instant lasagne sheets
50g Edam cheese, grated

METHOD

Brush a 30 x 20cm baking dish with melted butter or spray well with olive oil spray.

Heat the butter in a large pan and add the flour. Stir over low heat until the mixture is lightly golden and bubbling. Gradually add combined milk, sour cream and pepper to the pan, stirring between each addition until mixture is smooth. Stir constantly over medium heat for 5 minutes, or until the mixture boils and thickens. Boil for another minute then remove from heat. Stir in cheese and cool slightly.

Gradually add beaten eggs, stirring constantly.

Pour a third of the sauce into another bowl and reserve for the topping. Add pesto and carrots to the remaining sauce, stirring to combine.

Preheat oven to 150°C. Beginning with 1/3 of the carrot mixture, alternate layers of carrot mixture with sheets of lasagne in prepared dish. Use three layers of each, finishing with lasagne sheets.

Spread reserved sauce evenly over the top and sprinkle with extra cheese.

Set aside for 15 minutes before cooking to allow the pasta to soften. Bake for 40 minutes or until sauce is set and golden.

❋ Leave 15 minutes before slicing and serve with a green salad.

celebrate spring salads

Food isn't just about cooking – it's also about appreciating quality produce. There is no better time to encourage or reawaken this passion than in spring or early summer. Fresh splendid strawberries appear at my Sunday morning market at this time, as well as affordable bundles of slender, fresh pristine asparagus. The sensuous curve of the buds on a bunch of chives and the fresh aniseed aroma of chopped dill lifts and stirs the heart of a keen food-lover, reminding us all of the simple joy of eating what's in season and doing as little as possible in the way of preparation. This can never be overstated.

It's time to welcome new growth in the vege garden: the clusters of spring greens, rows of soft lettuces, sturdy vigorous ruby-red rhubarb and generous clusters of herbs such as parsley and mint make an energetic display. At the same time, it's appropriate to clean up all those favourite squash and root vegetables in the refrigerator and pantry to make way for fresh tomatoes, snowpeas and broad beans.

On a perfect spring day there is no need for mucking about in the kitchen with complicated sauces. If it's sunny, the garden or beach beckons so don't fret over weights and measures; get the basic principles right and let the produce do the talking!

CAPSICUM, SMOKED CHICKEN AND PAWPAW SALAD

This is a versatile salad and an excellent example of how the eye–appeal as well as the crunch and flavour of a salad is so important. The red capsicum, the savoury notes of the smoked chicken and the fresh, bright flavour and colour of the pawpaw bring a sweet note to the salad. Smoked chicken and pork love an association with pawpaw. You can substitute with mango or melon if desired. Add fresh herbs of your choice, from the last of the basil through to the zippy addition of coriander – this salad behaves well under all conditions.

1 red capsicum, deseeded and thinly sliced
1/2 pawpaw, deseeded, skinned and sliced
1/2 bunch spring onions, finely chopped
1 smoked chicken breast, skin removed and diced
3–4 handfuls of salad greens of your choice – baby spinach works well
toasted walnuts (optional)

METHOD
Mix all these ingredients together just prior to serving the salad.

✳ Drizzle with buttermilk dressing.

BUTTERMILK DRESSING

1/3 cup mayonnaise
1/3 cup buttermilk
1 tsp finely grated lemon peel
1 tsp lemon juice
1/4 tsp salt
1 tsp horseradish

METHOD
Combine all ingredients together.

✳ You can add freshly chopped herbs to this dressing. If you want more heat add extra horseradish and if preferred, add finely chopped fresh chillies.
✳ A little liquid honey, minced garlic and a tablespoon of Dijon mustard also works well instead of the horseradish.

SPRING BITES

✳ Rhubarb and cheese – a perfect finale to a glam lunch or dinner. Find some vine-ripened raisins (otherwise known as muscatel raisins) and place on a plate with 2 thin wedges of room-temperature brie, and to one side serve a small mound of poached rhubarb chunks (minus most of the syrup). The secret is to cook the rhubarb gently in sugar syrup just enough so the rhubarb is still intact, and then leave to cool.

✳ Celebrate new season's herbs – combine coriander with avocado for a spring green-looking snack. Chargrill thin slices of French bread or sourdough and top with a purée of avocado, lime juice, a dash of olive oil, green pepper Tabasco sauce (jalapeno sauce) and salt and pepper. Top the avocado mixture with a sprinkle of fresh coriander. A little poached chicken and cumin would also be welcome on top of the avocado/coriander topping, or perhaps cooked prawns or crabmeat marinated in sweetened lime juice.

✳ Celebrate spring chicken with a chicken salad made with watercress or baby spinach or snowpeas or pea shoots. Place chunks of poached (cooked) chicken in a ginger marinade overnight. Combine 1 tsp minced garlic, 3 tblsp rice vinegar, juice of 1 lemon, 1 tblsp sugar, 1 whole clove (very finely crushed), 2 fresh kaffir lime leaves (very finely chopped, optional), a light pinch of chilli flakes and 3cm fresh ginger (finely grated and juice retained – solids discarded). Next day, remove chicken from marinade, add a spoonful of sour cream or crème fraîche to the marinade and season. Combine the chicken in a serving bowl with the washed and prepared spring greens of your choice, slices of tomatoes and thin slices of radish. Top with revamped marinade dressing.

✳ Cut the mustard with spring vegetables. Blanch your favourite spring greens, for example, asparagus, early courgettes, early beans or snowpeas, in boiling water, then set aside. In a wok or large frypan heat a generous knob of butter and add a generous spoonful of wholegrain mustard. Add drained vegetables, toss well and throw in a handful of chopped mint. Serve with chargrilled fresh fish or chicken.

✳ With my lemon tree groaning with fruit, it's time to make a citrus and vodka sorbet. Combine 2 cups caster sugar and 2 cups water in a saucepan and stir over a low heat until sugar dissolves. Bring to the boil and simmer for 5 minutes. Cool, then refrigerate until cold. Then combine sugar syrup, 1 1/2 cups lemon juice, 1 1/2 cups pink grapefruit juice, 200ml citrus vodka (Absolut Citron) and 1/2 tsp grenadine syrup. Freeze in your ice-cream machine.

✳ Make an avocado and chickpea salad – combine spinach, chickpeas, sliced avocados and hard-boiled eggs in a serving bowl. Drizzle over a creamy chive dressing made with the juice of 1 lemon, 3 tblsp milk, 2 tblsp crème fraîche or plain yoghurt, chopped chives and salt and pepper. Sprinkle salad with sweet paprika and serve with fresh bread.

✳ Serve fresh strawberries, washed and stem intact, with crème fraîche and lemon rind combined together in one bowl and brown sugar and cinnamon in another. You dip the strawberry in the crème fraîche and then in the sugar. Perfect with early-season berries.

SALAD IDEAS

✳ Wash and dry well any salad greens. Use a salad spinner or place greens in the centre of a clean tea towel, pull up the ends together and spin the greens around 'lasso' style to remove any extra water, then dress with salad dressing. If you find all the dressing ends up in the bottom of the bowl, rather than on the leaves, you have too much water left on the greens.

✳ Serve prawns and avocado with a grapefruit vinaigrette. Seafood, and in particular prawns and crabmeat with their natural sweetness, really enjoy an association with grapefruit dressing. Make your favourite vinaigrette but use grapefruit juice instead of vinegar and add some very finely sliced zest to the dressing as well. If the dressing has to sit for a few days add more grapefruit juice just prior to serving to revitalise it; citrus, of any kind, has that ability.

✳ Make a Tandoori chicken salad for a warming weekend lunch. Place chicken breasts in Tandoori mixture (curry paste and natural yoghurt with garlic) and leave to marinate in the fridge for a few hours. Remove from marinade and grill. While still warm, but not hot, slice the cooked chicken and combine with salad greens, thinly sliced red onion and fresh mint. Drizzle with a cumin dressing: combine 1/4 cup sherry wine vinegar, 3 tblsp Dijon mustard, 1–2 tblsp ground cumin, 1 tblsp curry powder and 1/2 cup olive oil. Serve with warm Naan bread.

✳ The Box Café in Auckland makes a delicious, substantial salad combining dressed salad greens served with warm roasted walnuts, diced roasted beetroot and slices of new potatoes. A slice of warmed goats' cheese is placed on the top and the salad is served immediately. Add a little orange (the perfect partner for beetroot) to the dressing, and for extra appeal top the warmed goats' cheese with a few shreds of fresh orange zest.

the humble spud

Celebrate the humble spud. If you ever felt potatoes were becoming too predictable, get busy making these rösti. A perfectly cooked rösti – crunchy, buttery and creamy inside – is one of my favourite bases for everything, from scrambled eggs and slow- baked tomatoes through to reheated stew or ragout.

* The type of potato you use is critical – forget Agria or floury potatoes used for great mash. Here we need a waxy potato like Desirèe to hold their shape when cooking. Also, the older the potato, the more likely it will be watery when cooked, as many of the starches that would otherwise absorb the potato's natural moisture will have converted to sugars, so it's best to avoid older potatoes.

* Water is the number one enemy of a good rösti. Grate the peeled potatoes, do not rinse, and squeeze out all the liquid from the grated potatoes. I do this by hand and then finally in a clean tea towel to remove any last liquid.

* Once you put the potatoes into the pan, you don't want to disturb them as they cook, so you need a pan that doesn't have hot spots. A thick, heavy-based pan works well.

* Use plenty of oil – you need enough to actually fry the outer layer of the potatoes.

* If you have a large frypan and want to make small rösti without the expense and trouble of investing in small pans, you can use greased egg rings for individual portions.

* Don't rush your rösti. Some recipes for rösti call for precooking potatoes in their skins one day, leaving them overnight in the fridge, and then peeling and grating them to make rösti the next day. Take care with this method so that you don't overcook the potatoes; when you precook them they should still be very firm otherwise your rösti will turn to potato cake consistency rather than a crispy rösti. When cooking the rösti – and clearly raw grated potato will take longer – do not rush the process. Adjust the heat so the outside browns fully but slowly, giving the inside enough time to steam to completion.

* You can make rösti ahead of time and reheat in a 180°C oven in a single layer on an oven tray.

CRISPY POTATO BITES

* Rösti makes a delicious side dish to a stew, chops, roast or even other vegetables – try them with braised cabbage to start early celebrations of St Patrick's Day.

* An individual rösti can become a meal with smoked salmon, mixed salad greens tossed in olive oil and fresh lemon juice, and a dollop of sour cream seasoned with chopped fresh dill, chives, grated lemon zest, salt and lots of freshly ground black pepper.

* A superb showcase for cooked seafood is a rösti topped with hollandaise and either crayfish meat, prawns or lightly cooked scallops.

* The perfect breakfast rösti - try with a fried or poached egg on warmed-up salsa, sour cream, a few slices of avocado and a shower of chopped coriander.

* At your next barbecue make a large rösti and serve slices topped with thinly sliced seared steak and tossed with rocket, moistened with good quality olive oil and a generous squeeze of lemon juice at the last minute.

* A great rösti dinner suggestion is to combine thinly sliced cabbage and onions braised in a little white wine and chicken stock, and serve with slices of pan-fried sausage on rösti. Add fresh thyme to the cabbage with some caraway seeds for extra flavour.

* You can combine the potato with other ingredients for a variation on a theme. For example, peel, grate and squeeze 800g Desirèe potatoes and combine with 1 cup shredded rocket and 2 tblsp flour. Cook as per usual - this rösti is ideal as a base for chargrilled prawns with a topping of herb yoghurt sauce.

* A perfect starter for a dinner - tender baby spinach leaves tossed in your favourite vinaigrette, with halved cherry tomatoes, crumbled blue cheese and crisp fried bacon or pancetta on top of a slice or individual serve of rösti.

* The word 'rösti' has been adapted to mean any form of crisp potato or kumara dish. You can peel a large kumara, cut it into thin strips using the vegetable peeler and then toss these strips in a bowl with olive oil, salt and pepper and a handful of Parmesan cheese. Place on a non-stick baking sheet and bake for 15 minutes in a hot oven at 220°C. Use as a base for slices of roast chicken and top with dressed salad greens.

CRISP ROSTI POTATOES

This is more of a process than a strict recipe. So use this as a guide and have fun! The ingredients are not expensive, so try to get this right – practice will make perfect. Even failures though will be delicious eating.

500g Desirèe potatoes
1–1½ tsp salt
generous grind freshly ground black pepper
3–5 tblsp vegetable or olive oil for frying

METHOD

Peel and grate the potatoes. Place in a large bowl and with both hands squeeze the liquid from the potatoes. Then place the grated potatoes in a clean tea towel and squeeze again. Season with salt and pepper. The potatoes may start to discolour but don't worry as it doesn't affect the taste.

To make individual rösti, heat the oil in a heavy-based frypan until really hot and drop the potato into well-greased egg rings in the pan, ensuring an even surface. Use a fork to make sure you have a layer about 1.25 cm thick. Adjust heat so the bottom isn't browning too quickly. Use a spatula to flip the rounds. Cook the other side until golden and the potatoes feel tender when poked in the centre with a knife. Drain the small rösti on paper towels before serving.

✳ If you are making one large rösti allow extra cooking time. You can either flip the rösti over or slide the rösti out of the pan onto a plate and then turn over and slide inverted rösti back into the pan and continue cooking. For a large rösti you need to allow 12–16 minutes cooking time on one side and 6–8 minutes on the other. Make the necessary adjustments for smaller rösti.

It's really time for fresh sweetcorn. Serve an ear of superbly fresh corn as the perfect starter for your next summer dinner get-together. Feeding friends the best food possible does not have to involve hours in the kitchen. Forget spun sugar baskets and choux pastry – keep things easy. Put out the butter, sea salt and the black pepper grinder, provide plenty of napkins or clean tea towels and get busy.

Friendship is best defined as the ease you feel eating ears of corn together. If your company is oblivious to your lip-smacking, finger-licking enjoyment of the sweetness of freshly picked corn and never refers to the buttery juices that drizzle down your chin – you have a true friend indeed. The addition of salt and pepper lifts all the flavour and you somehow wish summer could last all year.

Buying the freshest corn possible is ideal. Roadside stallholders, growers at flea markets and stores with high turnover are your best option. The husks should be clean and green; the silk tassels bright with no sign of dampness or matting and the kernels pale, plump, well-filled and milky, with no space between the rows. Avoid cobs with dark yellow kernels or older large ones that look tough and dry.

With fresh sweetcorn, time is of the essence – the briefer the span between picking and eating, the sweeter and more tender the corn will be.

You can make superb fritters with freshly shucked corn, or throw some kernels into cornbread to accompany a bowl of chilli. You can make a great pasta or rice salad with vibrant splashes of yellow, or make a corn salad with roasted chopped red capsicums, lightly cooked beans and a salad dressing with plenty of garlic and lemon juice. You can throw corn kernels into a Ziploc bag and freeze for soup and chowders during the winter. If you are having friends for lunch you can serve a salad of corn, red capsicums, beans and slices of avocado with leftover chicken or sautéed prawns, or better still, crabmeat. Just place on a bed of dressed greens and serve with chunky bread and a nice goats' cheese on the side.

'Sex is good, but not as good as fresh sweetcorn.'
GARRISON KEILLOR

* Slice the corn off freshly cooked cobs and combine with lightly cooked capsicum wedges and gourmet salad greens like frisée for a deliciously substantial salad. Slice the capsicum and soften in a pan with olive oil, add seasoning and a light splash of sherry vinegar. Drizzle the remaining juices from the pan over the salad.

* When selecting fresh corn, check the stem to see how fresh it is and lift back the husk to squeeze a kernel of corn. If juices pop out, you have fresh corn. To roast fresh corn, peel back the husks and remove all the silks. Pull the husks back again and place on the grill for a few minutes.

* If you can't use sweetcorn immediately, then keep it in plastic bags in the fridge for 2–3 days. Allow sweetcorn plenty of space – if the cobs are piled on top of each other, this tends to generate warmth and 'cook' the corn.

* Make your own creamed-style corn. Cook whole cobs of corn in boiling water for 8–10 minutes and then remove the corn from the cob with a sharp knife. Combine with crème fraîche and salt and

CORN AND POTATO CAKES

Delicious with barbecued salmon or roast chicken – even bacon and maple syrup! Serves 3–4

2 large potatoes
1/2 cup finely chopped green capsicum
11/2 cups fresh corn kernels, including the pulp scraped from the cobs (cut from about 2 ears of corn)
4 spring onions, finely chopped
2 tsp ground cumin
3 tblsp flour
2 tblsp butter
4 tblsp sour cream

METHOD

Peel the potatoes, grate them coarsely and squeeze them well, with the capsicum, between several thicknesses of paper towels or a clean tea towel to remove any excess moisture. In a bowl toss together the potato and capsicum mixture, corn, spring onions, cumin, flour, and salt and pepper to taste.

In a non-stick frypan heat 1/2 tablespoon of the butter over moderate heat until the foam subsides. Add 3/4 cup of the corn mixture, tamping it down with a spatula. Cook the corn and potato cake for 6 minutes, or until the underside is golden and crisp. Slide it onto a plate, cover and keep warm. Make 3 more corn and potato cakes in the same manner with the remaining batter and corn mixture. Spread 2 of the cakes with the sour cream, arrange the remaining cakes on top, and cut the corn and potato cakes into wedges.

SUMMER CORN AND ORZO SALAD WITH CUCUMBER FETA DRESSING

13/4 cups crumbled feta cheese
3 large cucumbers, peeled, seeded, cut into 1.5cm pieces (about 41/2 cups)
1/4 cup olive oil
1 tablespoon water
500g orzo (rice-shaped pasta)
4 cups yellow corn kernels (cut from about 4 ears)
1/3 cup plus 2 tblsp chopped fresh chives
1/4 cup chopped herbs
1/2 lemon

METHOD

Place 1 cup feta cheese, half of the cucumber, oil and 1 tablespoon water in a food processor. Process until smooth and season dressing to taste with salt and pepper.

Cook orzo for about 8 minutes in a large pot of boiling salted water until almost tender, stirring occasionally. Add corn and cook for about 2 minutes longer until pasta is just tender but still firm to bite. Drain pasta and corn and transfer to a large bowl. Add 1/2 cup feta cheese, remaining half of cucumber and 1/3 cup chives and toss to combine. Mix in dressing and chopped herbs. Squeeze over fresh lemon juice and season salad to taste with salt and pepper. Sprinkle with remaining 1/4 cup feta cheese and 2 tblsp chives.

---

pepper and place in a small saucepan or bowl, cover and microwave for a few minutes only. Check seasoning, and add chopped chives and parsley before serving. For even greater flavour, slowly cook a chopped onion in a frypan, add the corn kernels and a generous spoonful of sour cream or crème fraîche and cook on a high heat for 1 minute.

* Fresh cobs of corn work well on the barbecue. Peel back the husks from 6 corn cobs and remove any white silk threads. Soak the cobs in water for 5–10 minutes. Combine 5 tblsp olive oil with 1 tblsp Moroccan rub and 3 tblsp finely chopped parsley and brush over each cob. Pull back husks so that each cob is covered. Tie tops with string. Place on the barbecue and cook gently for 10–15 minutes, turning often.

* Make herb and corn couscous. In a small heavy-based saucepan cook 1 cup fresh corn kernels in 1 tblsp butter over a moderately high heat, stirring, for 1 minute. Add 1 tsp minced garlic and 3/4 cup stock, and bring the liquid to a boil. Stir in 1/2 cup couscous, remove the pan from the heat, and let the mixture stand, covered, for 5 minutes. Stir in 2 tblsp chives, a small handful finely chopped herbs and salt and pepper to taste.

* Corn makes a happy marriage with seafood. Home-made creamed corn is a delicious base for a seared salmon fillet, and a prawn risotto enjoys an association with corn and chopped chives and chopped parsley. Cook the corn kernels in the stock, then remove and set aside. Make the risotto as per normal and add the raw prawns to the cooked rice, then 2 minutes later add the corn and the herbs.

* Make garlic and corn mash. Heat 1–2 tblsp oil in a heavy-based frypan over medium heat and sauté 1 medium chopped onion for 5 minutes. Add 1 cup fresh corn kernels and garlic and sauté for about 5 minutes longer until onion is golden and corn is tender. Stir in 1/2 cup cream, 2 tblsp butter and 1/4 tsp saffron threads (optional). Bring to boil and remove from heat. Cover and let stand for 20 minutes. Meanwhile, cook 750g potatoes in a large pot of boiling salted water for about 20 minutes until tender. Drain well and transfer to a large bowl. Mash until smooth. Stir in corn mixture and season with salt and pepper.

lazy grazing

If your idea of a perfect night in with your friends involves watching a movie or sporting event and grazing on platters of food, then look no further. Tell your company to come as they are and pull out the cushions and have a great time ... entertaining should always be this much fun. Just think platters, platters, platters!

SPICY SUMMER SALSA

This is a delicious, low-fat taste pointer on any plate – perfect with barbecued beef or chicken.

1kg tomatoes, peeled, seeded, and finely diced
1 yellow capsicum, finely diced
1 green capsicum, finely diced
1 red onion, finely diced
2 cloves garlic, finely minced
3/4 cup coarsely chopped fresh coriander
1–2 tsps finely minced fresh chilli
1/4 cup olive oil
2 tblsp balsamic vinegar
1 tsp sea salt

Combine all ingredients in a bowl.

BACON-WRAPPED JERSEY BENNES WITH BLUE CHEESE DIP

Perfect grazing food ... I mean who doesn't love delicious, small potatoes. I would never buy a second-hand car from someone who said they didn't like spuds!
Serves 4–6

450g Jersey Bennes (or small gourmet potatoes)
12 rashers bacon
3 tblsp olive oil
2 garlic cloves, crushed
1 tsp fresh thyme leaves
1 tblsp chopped parsley

DIP
100g blue vein cheese, crumbled
3 spring onions, trimmed and finely sliced
250g crème fraîche
2 tblsp milk

METHOD
Steam the potatoes until just tender or boil in water for 5–6 minutes until tender.

Drain and refresh under cold water to stop additional cooking.

When cool enough to handle, wrap the bacon strips around the potatoes. You can stretch the bacon to fit more snugly around the potato by using the back of a knife. When necessary, cut the bacon strips in half.

Place on a baking tray. Mix together the olive oil, garlic, thyme and parsley and drizzle over the potatoes. Bake for 15–20 minutes in a 200°C fan oven until golden.

DIP
Mix the blue vein cheese, spring onions, crème fraîche and milk, and season with salt and freshly ground black pepper. Serve with the potatoes and cherry tomatoes for dipping.

❋ Make a batch of sweet and spicy nuts – place 150g each of cashews, peanuts, almonds, pecans and hazelnuts in a bowl and stir through 4 large egg whites until well coated. In a separate bowl combine 5 tblsp brown sugar, 1/2 tsp chilli powder, 2 tsp cinnamon, 4 tsp dried sage and 11/2 tsp salt. Mix well. Pour the spice mix over the coated nuts and mix until well coated. Place the nuts on a baking tray and bake in a preheated 210°C oven for about 20 minutes. Stir them around a little every five minutes or so until they become even in colour. Cool on the tray and store in an airtight container – delicious warm with a cold beer.

❋ If platter food seems too dainty for your requirements, make up a pot of pasta or a pan of risotto and serve in generous bistro-style bowls. Serve with a fork only.

❋ Make a chickpea purée and serve on a platter with tapenades, pesto, cheeses, raw vegetables, slices of salami, gherkins and croutes. Soak 2 cups chickpeas overnight in plenty of cold water. Drain and rinse the chickpeas. Place in a saucepan, cover with fresh water and cook for about 30–45 minutes until tender. Add salt at the end of the cooking otherwise the chickpeas will take longer to soften. Drain and process in a food processor with a generous squeeze of lemon juice and 3–4 cloves of crushed garlic. Drizzle in enough olive oil to give you a soft purée. Taste and season and serve with croutes or pita bread toasts.

❋ For serious sports watchers with a hearty appetite, serve a platter of sizzling marinated chicken drumsticks warm from the oven with a roll of kitchen towels for messy fingers. Combine 1/2 cup sweet Thai chilli sauce with 1/4 cup coconut milk, 2 tblsp lime juice, 1–2 tblsp finely chopped coriander, 2 tblsp chopped roasted peanuts and 2–3 tsp soy sauce. Combine and add chicken pieces and marinate in the fridge overnight or all day. Remove from marinade and cook as per normal. They work a treat!

❋ If grazing food has to include something in pastry, why not try Thai chicken sausage rolls? Combine 500g chicken mince, 1 tsp ground cumin, 1 tsp ground coriander, 2 tblsp sweet Thai chilli sauce, 2 tblsp chopped fresh coriander, 1 cup breadcrumbs and salt and freshly ground black pepper. Spread the mixture along one edge of two puff pastry sheets and roll up to conceal the filling. Place seam-side down on a tray lined with baking paper. Brush lightly with egg and sprinkle with sesame seeds. Bake at 200°C for 30 minutes or until golden and cooked through. Slice the rolls and serve with a rocket salad and sweet Thai chilli sauce.

❋ No matter what time of day, serve ham, egg and Gruyère cheese sandwiches. Spread 8 slices of thick, white bread with Dijon mustard. Heat oil in a non-stick pan, add 4 eggs and cook to your liking. Top 4 of the slices of bread with shaved ham, an egg and the Gruyère cheese and then place the lids on top. Butter the outside of each sandwich, top and bottom. Heat a frypan or sandwich maker and cook, with a heavy weight like a pan or a couple of tins to weigh down if necessary. When the cheese melts and oozes out from the sides, it's ready to eat.

❋ For dessert, continue the grazing theme by serving platters of fresh fruit with a hot chocolate dipping sauce, or make some slices and biscuits ahead and serve on a white platter with coffee. Make the slices small and easy to manage. An easy citrus-inspired apricot slice is always popular – melt 200g unsalted butter and add 1 can condensed milk. In the food processor grind a packet of round wine biscuits and add to the pot with the melted butter/condensed milk mixture. Add 2 cups finely chopped dried apricots and 2 tsp finely grated orange rind. Press into a Swiss roll tin lined with baking paper and spread thinly with orange butter icing, then refrigerate until firm.

WARM CHOCOLATE COCONUT TART

There is nothing nicer than an invitation to a good friend's home to enjoy great food and wine. Fine wine importer Jean-Christophe Poizat and his wife Di are the perfect hosts. Warm, hospitable, sympathetic and great conversationalists – dinner is a memorable event. This delicious tart is a recipe that comes from France and was perfected by Jean-Christophe's sister, Florence – a much-requested dessert. Serve this warm with a dollop of cream and wait for a marriage proposal!

1 23cm sweet short
 pastry-lined pie plate
200g cooking chocolate
4 eggs
175g brown sugar
200g coconut
100g melted butter

METHOD

Place the unbaked pastry-lined pie plate in the fridge. Letting pastry rest in the fridge or freezer will result in less shrinkage when cooked.

Heat the chocolate for 2–3 minutes in the microwave, stirring from time to time. It is far better to work in short bursts to avoid 'burning' the chocolate.

Place the melted chocolate in the unbaked pie shell. Beat the eggs and sugar, add the coconut and melted butter and mix well. Place on top of the melted chocolate and bake at 180°C for 30–40 minutes until set and slightly coloured.

RHUBARB BUTTERMILK LOAF

Buttermilk makes the lightest and moistest loaf imaginable. This loaf keeps well and freezes perfectly! Even if you are not a rhubarb fan, you will change your mind after a trying a slice of this.

11/2 cups brown sugar
2/3 cup vegetable oil
1 egg
1 cup buttermilk
1 tsp salt
1 tsp baking soda
1 tsp vanilla
21/2 cups flour
2 cups diced rhubarb
1/2 cup chopped nuts
1 tblsp butter, softened
1/4 cup sugar

METHOD

Combine the brown sugar and oil in a bowl and stir well until smooth. Stir in egg, buttermilk, salt, baking soda, vanilla and flour. Blend until moist. Fold in rhubarb and nuts.

Place half of the batter into a greased loaf pan. Combine butter and sugar until crumbly and sprinkle half over the batter. Top with remaining batter and finish off by sprinkling the remaining butter/sugar mix over the loaf.

Bake at 180°C for 50–60 minutes until a skewer inserted in the centre comes out dry. Turn out onto rack and cool before slicing.

✱ Do not use fan-bake with this loaf – use regular bake. And good news, it is so cake-like it does not require buttering or any additional treatment, so enjoy with a good cup of coffee.

POLKINGHORNE PINEAPPLE PIE

When I was a child living in Tauranga, as a special treat my mother would always ask what we wanted for our birthdays. My answer was always chipolotas with pineapple sauce, followed by Mrs Polkinghorne's Pineapple Pie. This was, at a tender age, the makings of a fine foodie, or perhaps more realistically, a genuine pineapple enthusiast. No matter, Mrs Polkinghorne was much more than a great home cook – she would encourage us all with our swimming at the local pool as well. Images of luscious pineapple pie and an energetic lady yelling at me to swim faster are somehow completely interwoven. **Serves 4–6**

PIE
125g butter
125g sugar
1/2 tsp vanilla essence
1 large egg
1 tsp baking powder
250g flour

TOPPING
625g tin crushed pineapple
2 tblsp cornflour
1/2 cup sugar
1/4 tsp salt
1 tblsp butter
1 tblsp lemon juice

METHOD
For the base. Cream butter and sugar and add essence. Add egg, mix well and then add dry ingredients. Roll out into a greased sponge roll tin and bake for 20 minutes at 180°C. Cool.

For the topping, combine the pineapple, cornflour, sugar and salt in a saucepan over a low heat and cook until thick and clear. Add butter and lemon juice. Pour over the cooked base, chill and cut into squares.

Enjoy with lashings of cream.

✱ My mother changed the recipe slightly and made it with a biscuit base. Crush a packet of round wine biscuits and mix well with 200g melted butter. Press into a greased flan tin and place the pineapple mix on top. Chill.

BAKED CUSTARD AND PEACH STREUSEL TART
Serves 8

PIE SHELL
175g (11/2 cups) flour
1/4 tsp salt
1 tblsp caster sugar
120g cold butter, cut into cubes
2–3 tblsp cold water

FILLING
700g canned peach halves
150ml sour cream
3 egg yolks
200g caster sugar (1 cup)
30g (1/4 cup) flour

STREUSEL TOPPING
60g butter
75g (1/2 cup) flour
60g caster sugar (4 tblsp)
1 tsp ground cinnamon

METHOD
For the pie shell, sift flour into a bowl along with salt. Add sugar and knobs of cold butter and work the butter with your fingertips until the mixture resembles breadcrumbs. Mix in the cold water to form a shortcrust dough. Wrap in cling film and rest for about 30 minutes in the fridge.

Roll the shortcrust pastry on a floured surface to 3mm thickness. Grease a flan tin and line the tin with the pastry. Cover pastry with greaseproof paper and fill pastry case with dry beans. Bake in the oven at 220°C for 20 minutes. This is known as blind baking.

For the filling, drain the syrup from the peaches and line the baked-blind pie shell with peach halves. Combine the sour cream, egg yolks, caster sugar and stir until mixed well, then slowly stir in the plain flour without overworking it – just until blended, no more.

Gently pour the filling over the peaches and bake for 20 minutes at 200°C until the filling is cooked to the half-way mark.

For the streusel topping, combine butter, flour, sugar and cinnamon, then work the mixture together with fingertips to resemble a crumble topping.

Sprinkle the streusel topping on the pie and bake a further 20 minutes until the topping is golden brown.

SUPERB CHRISTMAS PUDDING

This is a family favourite of mine and is best made ahead, wrapped in greaseproof and tinfoil and frozen in a plastic bag until Christmas Day. If you are not that organised, it is fine to make it just before Christmas. Either way, your family will love it!
Serves 8–12

1 cup currants
1 cup sultanas
2 cups raisins
1 cup chopped dried apricots
1/4 cup brandy
11/2 cups crushed pineapple
1 cup flour
1 tsp allspice
1 tsp cinnamon
200g butter
2 cups fresh breadcrumbs
3/4 cup brown sugar
2 large eggs, well beaten

METHOD

Place the dried fruit in a bowl, then pour the brandy over the fruit and leave to soak overnight. The next day stir in the crushed pineapple.

Sift flour and spices into another bowl, rub in butter and add breadcrumbs and brown sugar.

Alternatively, place the flour, spices, butter, breadcrumbs and brown sugar in a food processor and process until crumbly.

Stir the fruit mixture into the breadcrumb mixture and blend in the beaten eggs. Pour into a greased 5-cup pudding basin, cover with wax paper, followed by foil and tie on securely.

Place pudding basin in a large saucepan of boiling water and simmer for 5 hours, replacing water as necessary with more boiling water.

Remove basin from water and cool. Remove pudding from basin, wrap in new tinfoil and place in a freezer bag and freeze until Christmas Eve, or you can store in a cool, dry place and douse with brandy as desired.

When ready to serve place, pudding back into basin, give it an extra douse of brandy and reheat in a large saucepan of water. Allow 1–2 hours. You can reheat by microwave if desired.

Cut into small pieces and serve with brandy cream and warm custard.

JOAN'S TRULY SCRUMPTIOUS SLICE

Mrs Joan Stirling of Auckland wrote to me several years ago with her favourite festive treat. 'It is so wicked and sinful,' she said, 'one only needs to make it for a special occasion.' Special occasions are generous affairs at Joan's house so she whips up a double batch and makes it in her large meat roasting pan, cutting it up once it is set and keeping in containers in the freezer – it is a favourite treat for family and visitors.

1/2 tin condensed milk
1/4 cup brown sugar
50g butter
1 tsp vanilla essence
2 tablespoons golden syrup
250g Kremelta
4 cups cornflakes
1 cup coconut (optional)
4 tablespoons cocoa
1 cup icing sugar

Boil first 5 ingredients together for 1 minute, then set aside to cool.

Melt Kremelta and pour over remaining ingredients. Press half the cornflake mixture into a sponge roll tin and chill. Spread caramel over top then place other half of the cornflake mixture on top. Chill in the refrigerator and cut into small pieces.

* This is the basic recipe, but it doubles easily. A welcome present during the festive season!

APRICOT BRANDY TRUFFLES

Busy Auckland caterer Nicola Hudson helped
me make hundreds of these brandy truffles for
a brandy promotion last year and she so loved
the result that she couldn't stop making them.
No matter what time of the day or night, dear
Nic was making these brandy balls, until her fridge
groaned with the results. Her clients were equally
enthusiastic and they too were consumed with
great energy. Place truffles in a container and
wrap with plastic wrap – they keep so well in the
fridge. You have been warned!

2 1/2 cups round wine biscuit crumbs
1/2 cup sweetened condensed milk
1/2 cup fruit mince
1/2 cup chopped nuts
1/3 cup finely chopped apricots
1 tblsp cocoa
2 tblsp brandy
icing sugar for dusting

METHOD

In a large bowl stir together all the ingredients except
the icing sugar until well blended. Using about 1 rounded
tsp of the mixture at a time, shape small balls with your
hands and roll each ball in the icing sugar. Place the
balls on a baking tray lined with greaseproof paper and
refrigerate for several hours or overnight until firm. Store
in the fridge until ready to use.

✱ Make Parmesan and basil or rosemary wafers to accompany your glass of bubbles.

Combine 2 tblsp grated Parmesan cheese with 2 tsp shredded basil or rosemary. Place on a baking tray lined with non-stick baking paper and spread the mixture to form a flat disk. Bake at 200°C for 5 minutes. Cool on the tray.

to assist with last-minute panic attacks

✱ Another fun idea for canapés at Christmas is to place a little spreadable cream cheese mixed with a hint of wasabi on thickish slices of telegragh cucumber and top with manageable pieces of smoked salmon. Slices of pear are also delicious topped with room-temperature blue cheese slices and a hint of chutney or relish.

✱ Berries are my indulgence at Christmas. Fresh raspberries can feature in your old-fashioned trifle this festive season. Use a chocolate sponge (order one from the bakery) and generously scatter with fresh raspberries, lashings of custard and cream. Instead of sherry, use a little framboise instead and add slivered almonds. For an extra indulgence, mascarpone cream is also superb in a trifle instead of regular whipped cream.

✱ Start the Christmas breakfast or brunch with fresh raspberries or blueberries on French toast or buttermilk pancakes made with fresh berries, dusted with icing sugar and a dollop of mascarpone.

✱ For the antipasti platter visit the deli section of your supermarket. Stock up on shaved ham, marinated mussels, sun-dried tomatoes, salami, feta cheese, smoked sausage or smoked fish, olives and, if the budget allows, artichoke hearts. All these items can be clustered together on a large serving platter and served with crostini, bread or crackers. Even raw vegetables can be added to this selection. You are only limited by your imagination – serve what you enjoy!

✱ Seafood platters are always popular – a quick trip to the seafood supplier can see you bringing home everything from sushi to smoked salmon and marinated seafood. If you can, fire up the barbecue, toss some fish fillets in a rub and then cook lightly on the grill and serve with salad. Shellfish is delicious cooked on a hot barbecue – just grab a pottle of pesto from the supermarket and combine with plain yoghurt or sour cream and use as a dipping sauce for the seafood. Similarly, another dipping sauce is soy sauce combined with sweet Thai chilli sauce, a squeeze of lemon juice and a little chopped coriander.

✱ Cheese platters work best if the cheese is at room temperature and you only try to serve 3–4 cheeses at one time, for example, a wedge of blue, a Brie or Camembert and an aged Cheddar works well. Select some sweet wines or port to accompany the cheese and serve with a basket of crackers and fresh fruit in another bowl to one side. This cheese option also makes a great gift if you are invited to share Christmas dinner with others and are not sure what to bring. Try a wedge of blue or Cheddar with a slice of Christmas cake for an out-of-body experience.

✱ Get your guests working and never underestimate the appeal of the barbecue. Invest in some marinated steaks and good sausages (precook them in a pot of cold water brought to the boil and then drain) and whatever else you enjoy and get the assembled party to cook their own Christmas lunch. Supply tongs and aprons on arrival. Cold beer and wine available on the deck is an added incentive.

✱ Delegate the bringing of salads – suggest a warm Jersey Benne potato salad with mint vinaigrette, a Greek-inspired feta and tomato and cucumber number, a green salad drizzled with lemon olive oil and a hint of balsamic vinegar, and an orzo salad with chunks of freshly cooked salmon, blanched snow peas and asparagus topped with fresh herbs. And everyone loves kumara salad – ask the 'volunteer' to roast small diced kumara or pumpkin and then combine with an orange and curry-inspired dressing and top with fresh herbs and a few toasted cashew nuts. This approach will guarantee the host has a stress-free Christmas and all the guests feel involved. The feedback will be entertaining!

Christmas in Vienna

'Yes,' I said. Who wouldn't? Suddenly, glorious images flashed before me – wonderful music, romantic dancing, hot chocolate, polite and correct dancing partners (they call you Frau after they get to know you), wiener schnitzel, Vienna Boys' Choir, scrummy chocolates, the white horses at the Spanish Riding School, apple strudel, the movie *The Third Man*, more opera, the building style of Hundertwasser, frittatensuppe (beef consommé with shredded pancakes), Schönbrunn Palace, art collections, turn-of-the century coffee houses, Mozart, Sacher torte, the last vestiges and images of the Austro-Hungarian Empire – Vienna is one of the few cities in the world that both men and women intentionally still wear feathers in their hats! The idea was completely spellbounding, and, best of all, it would be at Christmas.

Vienna would be fully decorated in fairy lights and the atmosphere at the Christmas markets would be magical …

I had to get out my dancing shoes and white gloves, this was my kind of town.

'Austrians love to celebrate famous dead people,' said my dancing partner as we swirled around the floor. The Strauss was demanding a fast pace. This dance tuition (and etiquette class, if you feel inclined) with the perfectly mannered Herr Thomas Schafer-Elmayer, next to the Spanish Riding School in the heart of Vienna, is a must for anyone with a sense of humour.

The dance school was founded in 1919 by Herr Schafer-Elmayer's grandfather, a former officer of the Austrian Imperial Army, Herr Willy Elmayer von Vestenbrugg. Today it combines tuition in manners and dancing based on the traditional imperial system.

'If you are feeling giddy,' my partner whispered discreetly, as my eyes were crossing in confusion (jet lag and twirling around in circles is not recommended), 'let's turn suddenly the other way.' Such a manoeuvre stops the room going round and round but would eliminate most of our fellow dancers; it was worth a shot. They were all being far too serious about it all, anyway.

The dance class suddenly stopped, we got our certificates and were ushered out politely. We were advised we would have to improve if we hoped to make the top social event of the year – the New Year's Eve Ball. To have the honour and prestige of 'opening that ball', as they say, Herr Elmayer has to assess your ability to waltz. You have to pass a test. If you can't waltz and turn to the left – no way – you will be out on the street.

But they don't mind if you dance in the street, said our charming Herr Elmayer. I like this place. Underneath the correct form and formality, there is a great sense of humour and fun. Any city that celebrates coffee and cake breaks with such enthusiasm has to be well worth a visit.

✳ Vienna during the Christmas season is a great experience for New Zealanders. The sipping of hot spicy wine and eating Christmas treats at the Christmas markets has an almost child-like fantasy quality about it all.

✳ As soon as you arrive have a coffee and head off on the ringstrasse tram that circles the old city (Trams 1 and 2). This will give you a great perspective of the city. Check out the municipal buildings – even the police headquarters are impressive. A ride in a horse-drawn 'Fiaker' cab is recommended in the old city centre.

✳ Start your day with coffee, semmel rolls (delicious with local jams) and cheese, sliced cold meats and softly boiled eggs. Mid-morning coffee and cake break – after you have tried the apple strudel do try the fresh cheese strudel: superb. For lunch, goulash soup, wiener schnitzel and more strudel – try a slice of cherry or plum tart. Take time over menus in Austria – the list of dishes is a history lesson. Here you will see the extent of the former hotchpotch of states that made up the Austro-Hungarian Empire, for example, goulash from Hungary and pasta and rice from Italy. Then perhaps a cup of hot chocolate and pastry at a café will be the perfect end to the day.

✳ Vienna is safe, gentle and sedate. Walking the city at night is not threatening and even an early morning trip to the Nacht Market (underground: Kettenbruckeng) to see the local produce and flea market is easy to achieve by public transport and not to be missed.

✳ Allow a few hours to visit a coffee house. Not just a few minutes to throw back an espresso at the bar as you would in Italy, but rather sit down and place an order with Herr Ober (this is what you call a waiter in a coffee house, never his first name, the locals informed me), read the papers and watch the flow of coffee drinkers.

✳ Don't wait to be seated; you select a favourite spot and order your coffee. You may need to visit the cake table (where the morning's baking sits proudly awaiting inspection) to decide on what you will have with your coffee, but you do not have to order rich pastries. You can just order coffee and sit there writing postcards and letters, or reading a book – you will never be thrown out or encouraged to leave. It would be a pity not to try something to eat – for a 'lighter' alternative many cafés serve slices of gugelhupf, a Viennese marbled madeira cake, a simply delicious companion to coffee. Coffee and cake will set you back NZ$9–11 depending on the sweet treat you select.

✳ Consistently, one factor ensures success for a Viennese coffee house and that is the personality and commitment of the café owners. The locals are quick to tell you of Frau Hawelka's enthusiasm to find you just the right seat and her magical yeast dumplings served warm at 10.00 p.m. each night or perhaps the warmth and joy of the waiters at Café Dommayer. Also if you have time, don't miss an opportunity to meet the open and friendly Herr and Frau Staub at Café Sperl.

✳ Café Sperl, Gumpendorfer-strasse 11, wood panelled, and with polished wooden floors, is a listed building with original architecture intact, and complete with high moulded ceiling and draped arched windows. (to page 92)

WALNUT TART

Walnuts are used extensively in Austrian cooking and this tart is superb with ice-cream or just with a dollop of whipped cream.

PASTRY
1 cup plain flour
1/2 cup sugar
125g butter, softened
1 egg yolk

FILLING
4 eggs
1/2 cup brown sugar
1 cup golden syrup
3/4 cup plain flour
1 cup roughly chopped walnuts

METHOD
For the pastry, place all the ingredients into the bowl of your food processor and pulse until it forms a ball.

Roll out onto a floured surface and place in a greased 23cm pie plate.

Place in the fridge while you quickly prepare the filling.

For the filling, beat the eggs, then add the brown sugar, golden syrup and flour. Pour into uncooked pastry shell and place walnuts on top. Fan bake at 180°C for 30 minutes on the bottom shelf of the stove (for the pastry bottom to cook) or until set.

A rendezvous for artists and theatre folk since 1880, Herr Manfred Staub has been keeping an eye on this café for 30 years – he is the third generation of the Staub family associated with the café. His love of people 'with all their terrible faults' he jests, is the reason he still loves the business. He confesses to swilling back ten cups of coffee himself each of the six days he works there every week. Three billiard tables made by the court billiard-maker grace one area, and the newspapers are laid out in another. Not to be missed.

✳ Café Dommayer, Auhofstrasse 2, dates back to 1787. Make a memorable detour when visiting Schönbrunn – it's a 10-minute walk. Superb food here – don't miss their strudels. We enjoyed a delicious, full-flavoured lunch. Johann Strauss jnr played here and the window seats have a great view of passing shoppers – it's a warm and inviting resting spot. This café has strong musical traditions, with concerts held on a regular basis.

✳ Café Central, Herrengasse 14, today a tourist attraction in Palais Ferstl, but at the turn of the century artists, writers, journalists and radicals met here – Trotsky was a regular. Built in the grand style – absorb the atmosphere!

✳ Café Hawelka, Dorotheergasse 6, a student hangout and once popular with artists, intellectuals and radicals. Visit at 10.00 p.m. for the 'warme Buchteln', sweet rolls filled with preserves. Warning: at this café the old 'obers' or waiters, or the grandmotherly Frau Hawelka herself, may tell you where to sit (in-between the bun making!).

✳ Café Landtmann, Dr Karl-Lueger-Ring 4, a meeting place for actors, right beside the National Theatre. You will see this grand café as you travel on the ringstrasse.

✳ Demmel, Kohlmarkt 14, a ten-minute walk from the Imperial Palace and Stephansdom – try the hot chocolate here. This is considered the most famous bakery in Austria – it had the royal appointment to the Emperor in earlier times. Consume your strudel in fin-de-siècle elegance.

✳ Hotel Sacher, Philharmonikerstr 4, this historic sight has been serving the world-famous Sacher torte (a super-rich chocolate-peach cake) in red velvet elegance for years.

✳ Visit Trzesniewski, Dorotheergasse 6 (just opposite Café Hawelka) – a little sandwich shop that is a grand Viennese tradition, famous for its open-faced sandwiches and glasses of beer for lunch.

WALNUT ICE-CREAM

6 egg yolks
1/2 cup caster sugar
1/2 cup gin
1 cup maple syrup
1 litre cream
1 cup chopped walnuts

METHOD

Beat egg yolks and sugar in a large bowl. Slowly add the gin, then the maple syrup and then the cream, while still beating. You want this mixture to form soft peaks, no more. Fold in the chopped walnuts and place in ice-cream containers in the freezer overnight. This ice-cream does not need stirring; if soft peaks have been formed in the beating process, the walnuts will not sink to the bottom during freezing.

✳ You will be delighted with this ice-cream recipe – the gin keeps the consistency just right, it never gets too hard.

WIENER SCHNITZEL

(Crumbed Veal Schnitzel)
A classic Austrian speciality – serve with oven-roasted potatoes or, better still, a herb and dill pickle potato salad and mixed green salad. Perhaps add a little dried herbs to the breadcrumbs for extra flavour and always remember with this treatment of veal that you need to season the meat well. Here is the traditional recipe.

160g veal topside or rump
salt and freshly ground black pepper
1 cup flour
1 egg
1 cup breadcrumbs
vegetable oil for frying
2 lemon slices
parsley for garnish

METHOD

Cut the trimmed meat into butterfly steaks and flatten with a meat mallet no thinner than 6mm. Season with salt and pepper and toss in flour, then egg and breadcrumbs. Make ahead and leave to rest in the fridge for 1 hour (if possible) before cooking. Fry in hot vegetable oil until golden on both sides. Remove from pan and drain on kitchen paper towels to remove any excess oil and serve immediately. Garnish with lemon slices and parsley.

✳ Serve with parsley potatoes and a green salad.

Clockwise from left: ✳ The coffee service at Café Sperl. ✳ The Christmas market at Schönbrunn Palace, a feast for the eyes and the soul. ✳ The perfect start to the day – fresh semmel rolls, delicious preserves and great coffee. ✳ Apple strudel – crammed full of apple and dusted with icing sugar. ✳ Fresh doughnuts – the perfect excuse to visit the Nacht Market in Vienna. ✳ Fresh deli food invites you in. Smart and pristine window displays in elegant Viennese food stores. ✳ The aroma and sight of fresh baking is lifted to an art form in Vienna.

PENGUIN BOOKS

Penguin Books (NZ) Ltd, cnr Airborne and Rosedale Roads, Albany,
Auckland 1310, New Zealand
Penguin Books Ltd, 80 Strand, London, WC2R 0RL, England
Penguin Putnam Inc, 375 Hudson Street, New York, NY 10014, United States
Penguin Books Australia Ltd, 250 Camberwell Road, Camberwell,
Victoria 3124, Australia
Penguin Books Canada Ltd, 10 Alcorn Avenue, Toronto,
Ontario, Canada M4V 3B2
Penguin Books (South Africa) (Pty) Ltd, 24 Sturdee Avenue, Rosebank,
Johannesburg 2196, South Africa
Penguin Books India (P) Ltd, 11, Community Centre, Panchsheel Park,
New Delhi 110 017, India
Penguin Books Ltd, Registered Offices: Harmondsworth, Middlesex, England

First published by Penguin Books (NZ) Ltd, 2002
1 3 5 7 9 10 8 6 4 2

Designed and typeset by Athena Sommerfeld
Printed by Everbest Printing Co. Ltd, Hong Kong

ISBN 0 14 301840 X
www.penguin.co.nz